Tempting Fake

Tracey Morait

ISBN: 978-0-9558550-5-4

Published by K&T Mitchell, UK
Cover design: Keith Mitchell

For Elaine and Chris

By the same author:
Episode
Big Brother
Epiworld
Abbie's Rival

Goalden Girl Series:
Goalden Girl
Goalden Sky

One
Cherry

It starts with one simple word: 'Hello.'
My name is Cherry and this is my story.

They were sending me to boarding-school. Helton Manor was on the shores of Coniston Water in the picturesque, breath-taking Lake District. The lake was always calm, even in bad weather, disturbed occasionally by the odd boat and one of the pleasure cruisers skimming along, and in the water, you could see a mirror image of the beautiful, green-rolling hills as the sun sparkled on the surface like stars. On the other hand, for all its extravagance, the elaborate furniture, plush red carpets and expensive paintings, the school was less impressive. Mum gave me the hard sell on it, insisting it was one of the best and most exclusive establishments in the country and had a reputation equal to Roedean and Cheltenham Ladies' College.

'I've never heard of either of them,' I told her furiously. 'Why do I have to go to a bloody boarding-school? Why can't I stay where I am?'

'Mind your language, potty mouth.' Mum sighed. 'Your dad thinks Helton Manor will give you a better chance of getting good qualifications and going to university. His mother went there and he's eager to carry on the family tradition. It'll be hard work for you sitting your final GCSE exams in a new school, but you're bright and I'm sure you'll manage. You'll be starting the new school year and there'll probably be other new girls in the same boat.'

I found out much later she wasn't really happy sending me away to school at all. If she'd said something, I might have had the chance to win her round, change her mind. Not for one moment was I fooled by Greg's concern for my schooling.

'He's not my dad, he's my bleedin' stepdad,' I corrected her sharply, 'and he's not thinking of my education, he's itching to get me out from under his feet.'

Greg was the only son of Lady Milborne and became Lord Milborne on the death of his dad. His first wife had committed suicide – no surprise – and he had a son of his own, Jeremy, away at university. Mum had met Greg at Milborne Hall, where she'd been appointed housekeeper and luckily, the job came with a small cottage. We'd been unable to get our own place because of the long housing waiting-list, so for years we'd had to share my grandparents' small bungalow, the four of us living on top of one another in cramped and crowded conditions. Mum had lost her cleaning job at the local library and one of the library assistants suggested she check out the ads in *The Lady* magazine for live-in work. It was the happiest I'd seen her in ages and my school was a short bus ride away.

It was all good in the beginning and Mum was an instant hit at the Hall, which had been built in the 1800s and had its own, beautifully-kept grounds on the outskirts of our town, old on the outside and dated on the inside, all wood panels, chandeliers and flash furniture. The cottage was cosy and my room lovely. My classmates were dead jealous and that skank Lacey Connor, thinking she was the toughest girl in the school, tried to bully me, saying Greg Milborne must've fancied Mum to give her the job. According to Connor, he had a reputation in the town for sleeping around.

'Don't judge other people by your own dirty standards, Connor!' I advised, pushing her head down the toilet and earning us both a visit to the headmaster's office for interrogation and subsequent detention. Despite me and my two best mates, Precious and Suze, not being part of the hard crowd, we took no shit from Lacey Connor. She gave us a wide berth after that, and she and her gang of trolls left me alone. I told no one about the wedding, except Precious and Suze, and that was weeks later.

Fortunately, it was a quiet wedding; a few select guests were invited and no announcement put in the paper. Nor was I required to be a bridesmaid, going to school while they tied the knot. Greg's mother was also absent, turning her snotty nose up at the idea of Mum becoming the next Lady Milborne.

Although he had Jeremy, Greg was no lover of kids. It was obvious from the beginning that I was a nuisance, an added responsibility to cast off, and he was adamant it was expected for the stepdaughter of a lord to be sent away to school. He had sent his seven-year-old son to Harrow and now it was my turn.

A younger edition of Greg, Jeremy Milborne came home from university to play the role of best man. Both men were tall and blond and had the same arrogant air and affected, upper class accent. Jeremy threw his rucksack on the floor and collapsed on the sofa.

'Is this her, Pops?' he said to Greg, surveying Mum critically. She went uncomfortably red. 'Not bad compared to the dogs you've dated in the past.' He turned to me, licking his lips and winking. 'The daughter's not bad, either.'

Urgh, what a creep!

I wondered how much of what Lacey Connor had said was true; it probably was of Jeremy Milborne. Both men were conscious of this leggy, fully-developed sixteen-year-old girl, showing off her slim legs in a short school skirt and a blouse not fastened to the top, the general school trend. I caught them both checking me out occasionally and that was the reason why I began to go round in baggy jeans and sweatshirts. Thankfully, two days later, Jeremy buggered off back to uni and I was safe.

Maybe boarding-school was a good idea if it got me away from Greg and his lecherous son. It'd be a waste of breath telling Mum she was marrying a perv and a paedo, she wouldn't believe me and anyway, she was besotted. He was promising her the world and it was the least she deserved. I couldn't deny her that by standing in the way of her making a better life. She was welcome to it. For all its comfort and opulence, Milborne Hall was a depressing place. I got the impression that if anyone at the Hall was unhappy Mum was marrying Greg, they were unwilling to say anything and hurt her feelings. Did they think she was too good for Greg? I certainly did.

Servants weren't a thing at the Hall, they were staff, and everyone was on first-name terms: no one called Greg 'Sir' or 'Your Lordship', he was Greg and Mum was Cheryl. Tulip, originally from Swansea in Wales and an art student at the local university, distinctive by her short dark hair, ring in her nose and tattoos on her arm, lived and worked part-time at the Hall to help pay for her course and had been assigned to wait on me. Whatever I needed, I called her, and in the few weeks I'd been at Milborne we became really close.

I loathed the Helton Manor uniform: the green tartan skirt, mauve blazer and hat, dark green sweater, white blouse and mauve tie. Greg had bought it from an exclusive school outfitters in London, no expense spared.

'It's really smart!' he commented during the fashion show I gave him and Mum, smirking slightly at my size 36C boobs that caused the buttons of the school blouse to gape a bit. I blushed, alarmed by the heaving of my chest and the thrill of his gaze. Greg was a sod, but he was a bloody sexy sod, tall, athletic, fit, a bit younger than Mum at thirty-six (she was thirty-nine). Imagining him and Mum doing it disgusted me; all the same, I struggled to get that image out of my mind.

I took no chances, avoiding him at every opportunity, locking my bedroom door at night and ensuring we weren't alone in the same room. Boarding-school guaranteed a safe distance between us. I loved my mum and was also annoyed at her for taking the job, for meeting him, and for him separating us.

On the Saturday I left for Helton Manor, a mild September morning, I hugged Tulip goodbye and we promised to ring one another regularly for a catch-up. My case was stashed in the boot of Greg's Mercedes, my trunk having already gone ahead by special courier, and I climbed into the back seat; he was driving me and Mum up to Cumbria. Having only seen photos of the school in the prospectus and on the website virtual tour, Mum was keen to inspect the place in person. I was dressed in the uniform, the stupid school hat and blazer on the seat next to me. Greg was in the driver's seat, waiting for Mum to finish faffing around in the kitchen, giving him the opportunity to gawp at me in the rear view mirror. Embarrassed by this unwelcome attention, I decided to get my own back by teasing him. I was wearing long black socks to my thighs and I crossed my right leg over my left, rubbing my hand over the top of my sock and letting my fingers roam up my skirt. He panted heavily, forcing himself to calm down at the sound of the passenger door opening and Mum getting in. He coughed and turned away. Grinning, my hand left my thigh and went to my hair to push it casually behind my ear.

'Forgot the sandwiches,' Mum said, handing me the lunchbox. 'It's your favourite, love, ham and cheese.'

'Cheers, Mum.'

Greg glanced at me again in the mirror and once Mum's back was turned I winked at him, and he hastily switched on the engine.

We had a break at the services on the M6 for lunch. Mum had prepared enough sandwiches to feed the five thousand; Greg preferred to order burger and fries from Burger King. Mum nipped to the toilet and I stayed in the car to log on to Pictapost and message Precious and Suze.

That morning, I'd posted a pic posing provocatively in my new uniform, jazzing it up by opening the blouse to my cleavage and revealing part of my lacy white bra, rolling over the waist of my skirt to shorten it enough to reveal the legs of my white knickers. My tie was wrapped round my neck, resembling a noose, giving the impression I was being sent to the gallows, and my hat sat at a jaunty angle. I had over nine hundred 'friends' and the post got over two hundred Likes, mainly from men sending love heart emojis and kisses, telling me how beautiful I was. The direct messages they sent me were blocked without hesitation. No-marks, saddos and catfishers swamped Pictapost and I enjoyed having power over them, drawing them in and letting them down. It was more Pictapost being the 'in' app than the attention and everyone, me and my mates included, used it. The direct messaging was free, cheaper than texting and better than Whatsapp.

Precious and Suze were missing me already and I was missing them. The last day at my old school had been full of emotion, tears, hugs, presents, promises to stay in touch and good lucks from teachers and pupils. I spent that evening in floods and nothing Mum said or did was of any consolation. Precious and Suze sent messages full of cry emojis and hopes I got sent away from Helton Manor. The problem was, if that happened, I'd end up back at Milborne Hall.

I tapped my message, thinking I ought to have tried harder to stand my ground against being sent away and insist I move back to Gran and Granddad's; they weren't Greg's greatest fans, either. At least I'd be able to visit Mum and go to my old school. I did have an uncle, Mum's older brother Andy; unfortunately, he lived in Germany. I also had a dad lurking somewhere on the planet and had heard nothing from him since he'd walked out on us fourteen years ago. I asked Mum what his name was and she'd said, 'Don't mention That Man to me!' and that's what I called him: That Man.

Not that standing my ground was an option, Greg said I had to go to boarding-school and that was that. Unless I got booted out, and if that happened I'd pack my bags and move back to Gran and Granddad's.

For the rest of the journey, I ignored Mum and Greg and read through my mates' wild ideas of how to get kicked out, adding a few of my own to lighten the mood. Murdering Miss Panesar, the headmistress, was one, albeit rather extreme. Setting fire to the gym was another over-the-top suggestion, whereas smoking in my room was a bit tame and besides, I loathed the smell of fags. Smuggling booze into class was a possibility and so was the danger of ending up in hospital getting my stomach pumped if I drank too much of it. Determined not to be put off, I geared up to get a reputation to be a nuisance and a troublemaker and surely they'd get tired of me and send me packing?

We arrived at our destination early in the evening, driving through the small, pretty town of Helton from where the school got its name. The shops and the solitary pub, The Jolly Miller, were built out of grey stone; a cross in the centre of the square had a poppy wreath resting against it and people were going in and coming out of an open Tesco Express. The school was situated on the edge of the town, past the train station. Its clock tower came into view above the trees surrounding it, the clock showing nearly ten-past seven. We were welcomed by large iron gates, our way blocked by a barrier and a security guard checking the car registration, my school ID badge and ticking my name off a sheet of paper on a clipboard. The barrier was raised and we soon reached the car park where eight cars were parked, presumably belonging to the teaching staff. I scowled at the building, built from similar grey stone to the shops in the town, wishing I was elsewhere.

Greg pulled up outside the big red doors. He and Mum got out of the car and I stayed in my seat, gripping my phone, a million things passing through my brain: if they tried to get me out, I'd scream, convince Mum that Greg had been looking at me in a funny way, she'd tell him it was over and we'd catch the train home, away from Helton Manor, away from Greg. They'd get a divorce and I'd be free of him forever.

The back passenger door opened. Greg said, 'Come on, Cherry,' and I meekly unbuckled my seatbelt. He opened the boot to take out my case.

Mum was approached by a young, smartly-dressed woman, her blonde hair tied in a ponytail, wearing a tight-fitting grey skirt, beige blouse and black stiletto shoes. She was in her early twenties and offered her hand to Greg, who seemed reluctant to let go. Politely and firmly, she released his grip.

'I'm Joely, Miss Panesar's secretary.' She turned to me and smiled. 'Cheralyn Hill?' I winced and nodded. I detested people using my full name. 'Welcome to Helton Manor. We're glad to have you. Miss Panesar is waiting to meet you and I'll take you to her office shortly. Rowan is the building next to this one, where you will be boarding.'

Five minutes later, we reached a smaller, more modern red-bricked building. Inside, the walls were painted white, giving it a more inviting and cheerful appearance.

'Joely,' I said shyly, 'do you mind calling me Cherry? OW!' Mum nudged me warningly.

Joely laughed. 'Cherry it is; however, you'll find Miss Panesar and the teaching staff will call you by your full name. Now, some information: the juniors sleep in six bed dorms over in Willow, that's the building next to this one. You older girls have study bedrooms here in Rowan, four to a room. Next year, in Year Twelve, you'll move to Oak Sixth Form House, where you'll share two to a room. You'll get a proper tour of the school and grounds tomorrow and we provide maps! Your roommates will buddy you for the first month and help you settle in. Your trunk has arrived and you can unpack later. Shall we take the lift? You're on the second floor.'

During the lift ride, Mum said, 'Where are the other girls?' She squeezed my hand tightly. The place was eerily quiet.

'Supper finished ten minutes ago and most of them will be in the common-room relaxing,' replied Joely. 'A few have gone home to visit their families for the weekend.'

The prospect of going home every weekend appealed to me until I realised forlornly there'd be a cost to the train and coach tickets. The chances of Greg coming up every week struggling through Friday night traffic to pick me up were zero, and what if he came alone?

'Weekends are fairly free and easy here,' went on Joely, breaking into my thoughts, 'and there's plenty to do; walks, the cinema, games, dancing, the odd party, going into Helton – there's a very popular coffee shop the girls frequent called the Country Kitchen. I'll also give you a list of clubs to join. Everyone has to be back in school by six for supper and no girl is allowed out of the grounds in the evenings, unless accompanied by a prefect or member of staff for a specific reason – ah, this is you, Cherry.'

At the sight of the white door and the brass number 5 fixed to it, my stomach turned somersaults and Mum's ham and cheese sandwiches were in mortal danger of shooting up all over the floor. Joely knocked first. No answer. She opened the door to an empty, quite cosy room, where the bookshelves were cluttered full of textbooks and novels. Stuffed toys and fancy cushions littered three of the beds, one under the window and the others by the walls. Each bed had a side set of four white drawers next to it. My trunk was resting on the tidiest bed and Greg dumped my case next to it. I admired the magenta duvet and magenta pillowcases, and the window had a magenta blind pulled down halfway, overlooking the car park and grounds beyond.

'Suki, Rahma and Tasha are your roommates, Cherry,' said Joely. 'They're probably in the common-room watching a film on Netflix. You'll meet them later.' Her mobile phone buzzed. 'Ah, it's a text from Miss Panesar. Come on, we have to go back to the school building to her office.'

On the inside, the main school building was how we remembered it on the virtual tour and reminded me of Milborne Hall. The high white ceiling in the hallway had two large chandeliers, real crystal, probably; the fees they charged a term were astronomical enough for them to afford such decorations. The wall lights, already switched on in spite of the large windows letting in the daylight, had brass fittings and ornamental glass shades.

Miss Panesar's office was an impressive room on the ground floor, dominated by a large mahogany desk and lamp, paintings on the walls and thick, white, rose-patterned curtains on the window. I recognised her from her photo in the prospectus: tall, slim, brown eyes and brown hair greying at the temples. She was a bit older than Mum, probably in her forties, and dressed in a tracksuit.

'Hello!' she said enthusiastically. 'Forgive the informality; I'm off to the gym for a game of squash shortly.' We shook hands. 'Welcome to Helton Manor, Cheralyn. I hope you'll be very happy here. Please,' she indicated the armchairs, 'take a seat and I'll go over a few things...'

I paid no attention, allowing my mind to wander and imagining being a million miles away. At last, the interview was over and I was escorted back to Rowan House by Joely to unpack and meet the other girls.

'Your parents can help you get your things organised, Cherry,' she said. I liked her. She was nice and saw how uneasy I was being away from home. She put her hand lightly on my arm. 'Otherwise, you may find it's best to say goodbye now. It's up to you. Everyone here, including me, was new at first. On my first day, I found it easier in the long run to get the goodbyes over sooner rather than later, rip off the plaster. I can guarantee it's the best remedy and your homesickness will pass faster than you think.'

I decided to rip off the plaster. The longer I left it, the harder it would be and Greg was nagging at Mum.

'We have to get going, Cher.'

Yeah, bye, Greg, I'll miss you. Not.

Stepping out into the drive, I said in a wavering voice, 'You get off, Mum. I'll be fine, honest.'

I acted more confident than I actually was. Three whole months stuck in this dump! What a rotten swine Greg was!

'Come here, you.' Mum collected me in a big hug and the tears coursed down my cheeks. She kissed me and cupped my face in her hands, trying hard to hold on to her own composure. 'Now listen, if you're not happy…'

‘Come on, Cher,’ called Greg impatiently from the driver’s seat. ‘I need to fill the car with petrol and get home by midnight.’

Mum kissed me again.

‘‘Bye, love,’ she whispered, and I waved until the car was completely out of sight.

Two
Adam

It starts with one simple word: 'Hello.'
My name is Adam and this is my story.

I'd fallen in love. Her name was Cherry, also known as @cherryhillpie on Pictapost, and she was gorgeous. Whenever my mood got spoilt – and that happened a lot – I ogled at the last picture she'd posted, my favourite, in her school uniform, her blouse unbuttoned, showing a nice bit of cleavage and the tie around her neck. My mouth watered; how I'd love to get my hands on her! She was sixteen, older than me by a few months; nevertheless, I knew how to show her a good time!

I sighed, lying back on the grass and staring at the sky dreamily, resting the phone on my chest. Sadly, she was out of reach. She was moving up to the north of the UK to a school in the Lake District and I was at a school down south in a place called Suffolk, located on the edge of the small village of West Somerholt, a million miles away from my home in New Jersey. I loathed England, West Somerholt and The Priory School. I was there because my dad, a captain in the US Air Force, had been stationed nearby at RAF Garforth for five years and my English mom was intent on me having a good education at a top British school. Her dad had been a teacher at The Priory years ago and it was therefore her choice, having no confidence in the local school where most of the other kids from the base went. I'd been at The Priory for two semesters (terms they called them here). Mom said I had to learn British English to fit in. I was a weekly boarder, going back to the base at weekends. Dad said it was best for me to board to help me to learn to live independently and to keep me in line. I'd been thrown out of high school in New Jersey for fighting. The Priory's regimented rules suited him and it was a passable alternative to the military school in the US he'd rather have sent me to. Fortunately, Mom was less eager than I was for me to suffer the fate of marching and parades before breakfast.

Being the solitary American at the school, I had no pals and the others called me The Colonial, not by my real name, Adam Fisher. I hated them singling me out; was it racism, culturism, maybe, if that was a thing? I had no idea. I was equal to my fellow students; the problem for me was they were sons of lords, sirs and dukes, and those from overseas, India, Africa and Europe, sons of princes and barons. Like most Americans, I traced my ancestry to Ireland, a descendant of Irish farmers from the potato famine, joining many others to sail across the Atlantic and seek a better life.

The tap of a foot against my thigh ruined my delicious daydream where I was enjoying the company of the luscious Cherry. Mr Jenson, the sports teacher, was standing over me in his black tracksuit, frowning.

'Found you, Fisher!' he growled. 'Why did you leave the pavilion? Come on, everyone's waiting. You're in.'

I blinked. 'In what?'

'In to bat, you muppet! Singh's been bowled out for thirty.'

Grunting irritably, I dragged my weary bones off the grass. Cricket! Of all the cockamamie sports in the whole wide world, it was cricket! Rugby was another one and if I dared call their football game 'soccer' they almost had a fit. It was actually rugby and soccer semester, but the September weather was warm enough to get a few cricket games in. The authorities were intent on taking advantage of late fixtures that had been postponed during the summer for whatever reason, and here I was, a fish out of water, dressed in these dumb cricket whites.

I picked up the flat bat thing from the grass and plodded behind Jenson past the fielders, all standing and gawping at me irritably, arms folded. At the crease, Petrov was in front of his wicket, swinging his bat and nattering to the wicket-keeper from the opposing house. Seeing us approach, they nudged one another and Petrov said, 'Oh, it's you! We were laying odds you'd flown back to America!'

If there was one thing that irritated Dad it was the number of Russian kids The Priory had, sons of rich oligarchs. Daniil Petrov was very popular and I envied his good looks: the black hair and astonishing dark brown, almost black eyes that narrowed in a sinister kind of way, flawless pale skin and his constant smug, almost shady manner. He was easy to detest and the feeling was very mutual.

'Come on, Fisher, get a move on, and take your place at the crease!' snapped Jenson.

'Why do I have to play this stupid game, sir?' I grumbled back at him. 'We don't have cricket in the States.'

'It's enough for me you can bat.' My talent at handling a cricket bat had turned out to be equally a surprise to me than it had to everyone else; I hadn't played baseball that much back home. On the other hand, my fielding skills weren't highly commended. I was no all-rounder. 'You're almost good enough for the Second Eleven, if you sorted that temperament of yours.'

Grumbling, I stood in front of the wicket, grasped the bat handle, and waited. Further down the field, the bowler was rubbing the ball down his trouser leg and creating a red streak, another weird ritual of this game. He ran towards me, tossing the ball in his right hand; it bounced just short of me and I walloped it. It flew towards the pavilion and Jenson put both hands in the air to indicate the six runs. Claps of appreciation rang in the air and I waved my bat at them in thanks.

Twenty minutes later, I'd achieved twenty more runs. Jenson removed the bails from the wicket to mark the end of the match.

'Stumps! Stanthorpe House wins by fifty-three runs.'

Our opponents, Gregory House, gave the customary three cheers and on the way back to the pavilion, Jenson said, 'Well played, everyone. You've all given me fair consideration for the team selections next month; you, too, Fisher.'

'The Colonial, sir?' said a boy called Freddie Carlton-Greene. 'Fours and sixes are fair enough, 'cept he's no fielder and…'

'Neither are you, Carlton-Greene,' interrupted Jenson pleasantly. 'Kindly leave the team selection to me.'

I had little chance of being chosen for the team, anyway, and Jenson was right: Carlton-Greene was physically unfit for team sports, getting by in cricket on singles and twos and rarely selected for rugby. He was often bowled out early and was nearly always assigned to wicket-keeper in the field.

Once showered and changed, I wandered into tea and an hour's prep, boarding-school speak for homework, supervised and held in a study room. Either a prefect or teacher kept guard, whoever drew the short straw. Cell phones (mobiles the British called them) were forbidden in prep and class, which by no means prevented any of us sneaking them in, of course. The standard of work here was different to what I was used to back home, especially in Math ('Maths, not Math!' the teacher often snapped at me), and it was a slow process catching up. Not that anyone had actually labelled me backward; it was more a case of being 'not quite suited' to the British way of education. This school's morals and its crop of hostile students was why I needed my phone, to touch base with my buddies in the States using the free Pictapost messaging.

I'd shared Cherry's latest picture and the reception was what I expected.

Hot!' @deano commented. I'd met Dean at school in New Jersey and he was a nice guy, keeping his promise to connect on Pictapost. I chuckled. Cherry wasn't Dean's type: he was gay.

'Gorgeous chick!' said @scott_dude. 'I'd take her to heaven and back!'

He was my best pal and in the same boat, being the son of an army captain. His dad was stationed in Germany now and he attended an American base school there. We'd been in a New Jersey elementary school together and parting had been difficult. We'd vowed to be friends forever and we'd meant it. I'd have done anything for Scott and vice versa. Cherry's pics and his messages kept me going in my solitary life in this peculiar British world.

Other dudes on Pictapost posted love hearts and red rose emojis on Cherry's profile. I was aware they'd friended her and were hoping she'd return the favour. None of my business; I had no claim over her and spoke to other girls on my list. They tagged me in their pics and I rewarded them by Liking. Cherry was the one giving me the hots, though, and I showed all of her posts to Scott and Dean. I hadn't messaged her. Scott had and she hadn't engaged. What if she rebuffed me and messaged other guys?

I hadn't realised, after finishing my Geography prep and waiting for the others to finish theirs, I'd moaned aloud at Cherry's uniform pic. All heads turned to me.

'Fisher?' Miss Emerson said. I looked up from my phone and watched her rise from her chair. *Oh, shit.* Hurriedly, I put the cell in my pocket and stood up.

'Ma'am?

She was a young woman of around thirty, plain and unattractive, not slim, nor fashionably dressed in a long yellow, rose-patterned top, black leggings and flat lace-ups. The boys called her Dumpling behind her back.

'I keep telling you not to call me "ma'am", Fisher. I'm not the Queen.'

Sniggers.

'Sorry, ma'am – Miss Emerson.'

She held out her hand. Tutting, I pulled the cell out of my pocket and gave it up.

'Thank you. The rules regarding phones during school hours are perfectly clear. You'll get it back at the end of prep.'

Thank God the screen had locked and she couldn't see Cherry's picture in all its glory. I sat down again, my cheeks burning, trying to ignore the haughty looks from the others. Most of them were on Pictapost and up to now I'd succeeded in dodging them. We had nothing in common and the last thing I wanted was for them to find Cherry's profile on my list.

Freddie Carlton-Greene turned and waved his phone at me. Emerson marched up to his desk and snatched it from him, causing the class to collapse into fits of laughter. Prep over, the others rushed out to their respective houses, leaving Carlton-Greene and me to stay behind to collect our phones, listen to a lecture and be awarded an hour's detention to be taken the next day.

Emerson finished telling us what she thought of us and added, 'Shut the door on your way out.'

We left the room in silence until, safely out of earshot, Carlton-Greene spat, 'That woman's a right bitch!'

'Yes.'

Petrov and Imran Aziz, Carlton-Greene's cronies, had hung back and were waiting by the statue of the school's founder, Sir

Hugh Stonebridge. Petrov was puffing at a vape, an illegal custom at the school to flout the rules against the ban on smoking. Petrov took no notice of rules and had been told he'd be permanently excluded if he was caught smoking again. 'Vapes don't count,' he insisted. His dad was a billionaire and owned a London soccer club. Petrov figured that gave him the right to do what he liked. He frowned at Carlton-Greene and me approaching. Aziz nodded to me and said nothing. The son of a Pakinstani diplomat, he was a decent dude and often said hi. Nor was he scared of putting the Russian in his place.

'The Colonial agrees,' Carlton-Greene said, 'Emerson is a bitch.'

'She always has been,' said Aziz.

Petrov gave me a long stare, took a final puff on his vape before tucking it in his jacket pocket and we walked towards Stanthorpe House in silence, me bringing up the rear and not realising Carlton-Greene was strolling behind me. I took out my phone for one final glimpse at Cherry, startled by Carlton-Greene grabbing it and crowing, 'Hey! Come and see the tasty bit of skirt the Colonial's following on Pictapost!'

Three
Cherry

Rahma Kandie, the daughter of a Kenyan chieftain, and Suki Ito, whose father was a Japanese politician, were both really nice, attractive girls: Rahma had flawless dark skin and beautiful, long straight black hair, and Suki had amazing large brown eyes, short spiky hair, gold highlights and an enviable slim figure. Tasha Kennedy, the other occupant of Room Five, a Londoner whose parents lived in Qatar, was quieter and not much of a talker. She always had a sulky expression on her otherwise pretty face. I was told the previous occupant of my bed, a girl called Essie, had died two terms ago and I was her successor. No one was prepared to tell me what had happened to her and it was almost as if I was wearing a dead girl's shoes. If I probed for information, they refused to discuss it, especially Tasha, and I decided not to mention it again, leaving me to imagine all sorts: she'd taken an overdose, died in her sleep, been run over by a joyriding Sixth Former. I trawled the internet for news of a sudden death at Helton Manor School without success. From what I gathered, nothing sinister had happened to her, and I found that to be a bit of a disappointment. It turned out Essie and Tasha had been best mates and that accounted for Tasha's moodiness.

'Tasha-chan really misses her and I understand it's natural for her to be depressed she's not around any more,' explained Suki in her refined English accent. 'Essie got Tasha and they were good together. Tasha's a very insular person and has few friends in school, apart from us, of course. Don't fret,' she added reassuringly, 'Tasha doesn't think you're an intruder and taking Essie's place.' That hadn't crossed my mind. 'She'll get used to having you around eventually.'

Suki said no more. Essie's story was clearly none of my business.

Apart from me, Rahma, Suki and Tasha, there were sixteen other girls in my year. Having arrived that Saturday evening and escorted to the common-room in Rowan House by Joely, I was formally introduced. The film was paused and ten curious girls examined me closely. I said a shy and nervous hello to Tasha and Rahma. Suki had gone to swimming practice; most of the others were home for the weekend or taking part in other activities. Joely left the room and the questions were fired at me from all angles:

'Where are you from?'

'How old are you?'

'What was the name of your last school?'

'How come you've arrived a week late?'

I was truthful, not holding back on the rags-to-riches story, adding the fact I disapproved of my mum marrying Greg and just stopping short of calling him a perv.

'Your mother was a cleaner and a housekeeper?' said the American girl called Clarissa Cleverley, ironic considering she actually had the brains of a peanut. She'd been kept down a year for flunking all her GCSEs, claiming the schools in the US were different to those in the UK. She'd been at Helton Manor for five years and everyone said it was lame for her to use her nationality as an excuse to be dim.

'Yeah, and now she's Lady Milborne,' I informed her, taking an instant dislike to this cretin. Having lanky, mousy hair and spots on her chin was no crime, the nasty laugh and general unpleasant manner was. Apparently, her mother was some British actress I'd never heard of and her father an American film director. They were divorced and Clarissa had chosen to live with him in America when she was home from school.

Being the stepdaughter of an English lord failed to impress my classmates, most of whom were the natural daughters of the titled and rich. I was obviously common, coming from a poorer background. Rahma and Suki were different: Rahma was kind and patient, correcting me on the school rules, whereas Suki was more abrupt and direct, not caring if she offended anyone. For all that, she was a generous, likable, good-natured person and very popular. Tasha was Tasha and I had to accept her for who she was. It was a bit early to say if we'd ever be besties, though. I missed Precious and Suze more than ever and I missed my mum more. Helton's rules got up my nose and I was fed up being told what to do by the prefects. I had no freedom and was homesick for my old life.

Since arriving at Helton Manor and being on my own, Pictapost became an obsession and it was no surprise I was more and more addicted to it. Apart from contacting Precious and Suze, posting and messaging Tulip became a lifeline. I loved hearing from her and we also used Whatsapp video and Snapchat to exchange news. I lied, telling her I was settling in and fed Mum the same fib during our conversations on the phone. Leisure breaks were the worst and I discovered another irritating rule Rahma kindly pointed out on my first day: although mobile phones and tablets were allowed outside class and prep, social media was banned, Pictapost in particular.

'They decided this term,' she explained. 'Miss Panesar announced they were ditching it at First Day assembly, just using Twitter to keep parents in the loop for news. Girls had been posting on Pictapost and tagging the school, and people – men and boys, mainly – left rude comments. It was a lot of aggro for the school to police and so they binned it.' Rahma avoided my gaze and I wondered whether she'd been one of those girls.

'Were they saucy, the pics?' Like the suggestive one I'd posted on the morning I'd left home? I hadn't tagged the school account, not realising there was one, but I had cited Helton Manor. 'I mean, short skirts and boobs and things?'

'Haven't got a clue,' said Rahma. 'It was mainly the older girls doing it and most of us defy the ban 'cos it's pissed us all off. If you do go on it, take care not to get caught surfing and posting stuff to draw attention to the fact that you're a pupil here and keep off the other social media sites if you can. If not, don't name the school, whatever you do.'

I huffed silently. *Was I ever going to have any fun at all in this place?*

For all Rahma's advice, the social media ban didn't prevent her, Suki and Tasha friending my Pictapost account and on seeing my uniform post, Rahma gasped, 'WHOO! Very risqué! And those comments! Lucky for you the badge isn't showing, it's bad enough the skirt and tie screams Helton. I'd delete this if I were you, Cherry.'

'I'll think about it,' I said hesitantly.

'Seriously, Cherry, I'd do more than that.'

Suki laughed and whistled and called me a hot chick. Tasha said nothing.

'I'll be careful how I use it in future,' I assured Rahma. 'I shan't give it up. I use it to keep in touch with my old mates, see.'

I lived for news from Precious and Suze; however, the weeks went by and their messages were getting shorter and shorter and fewer and fewer. I'd check my phone and sulk. They were forgetting me! Out of sight, out of mind!

Meaning one thing: I needed new friends.

Rahma, Suki and Tasha were my best bets and soon I began to fit in. I made my bed and space my own, bought cheap, colourful cushions and stuffed toys from a shop in the town, and gradually my life at the Manor morphed into a similar state to everyone else's, a home from home. I was a bit happier and my work, not great at first thanks to struggling to keep up, improved. The standard was much higher than at my old school and I had to pull my socks up and work hard for this final GCSE year, pass my exams, make Mum proud, so I had to abandon my plan of being excluded. I was determined to pull my socks up and work on my relationships at school.

Tasha was distant in comparison to the outgoing Suki and Rahma. She went round in a bit of a dream world of her own, obviously not yet over Essie's death. I sympathised, sensing her pain, even if, in my case, the loss of my mum was temporary.

I became very careful, logging on to Pictapost at break and in the evenings, relying on my virtual world for companionship. I decided not to delete the post of me in the Helton Manor uniform. I lapped up the glowing comments, craving the attention, and chose to delete the name of the school instead. Why not keep it online if it had more Likes than any of the other posts?

One morning, during a particularly low mood, I received a direct message from someone calling themselves @adamfishofficial. I was intrigued and opened it.

'Hello,' it said. 'I'm Adam. Are you lonely at your new school?'

I studied his profile and saw a handsome lad my age, attracted by his light brown hair, green eyes and the hint of stubble on his upper lip and chin. The scar above his right brow, apparently caused by a baseball, somehow added to his attraction. He'd posted four photos, selfies, two of him alone smiling, one of him and two other boys and another where he was standing next to a man in uniform, his dad, an American flag behind them.

The message was a high point in what had turned out to be a rubbish morning, having been verbally abused in Physics class, where I'd struggled to understand the hieroglyphics that bitch Mrs Sharma had scribbled on the whiteboard and showed me up in front of everyone by forcing me to write out the rest of the equation. Suki had warned me what a cow Sharma was and there was muffled sniggering during my embarrassment. Now it was break and I was alone; Rahma, Suki and Tasha were gassing to a group of girls from our year and had forgotten me. Ignoring my golden rule of not speaking to strangers online, I took a deep breath, my heart pounding, and wrote, 'My name's Cherry. How can you tell?'

I waited for the word 'Read' to show below my message and by the end of break it hadn't shown. On hearing the bell ring for the restart of lessons, I shrugged, logged out of the phone, set it to silent and put it away in my skirt pocket.

During English Lit and engrossed in *An Inspector Calls*, I briefly forgot Adam until my phone vibrated near the end of the lesson. The teacher turned his head away and I quickly read the Pictapost message.

'I'm also at boarding-school,' Adam had written. 'I have no pals here. Where are you from?'

WOW! A good-looking lad from America messaging me; where was the harm in that? My knowledge of America came from what I'd seen on telly. He told me he was from New Jersey, USA, and at school in Suffolk down south. At that moment, annoyingly, I had to log off for dinner; no way could I risk messaging him in a dining-room full of people.

I sat next to Tasha and she said unexpectedly, 'How are you settling in?'

I nearly dropped my cup of tea in surprise.

'Slowly,' I informed her truthfully.

'Yeah, it's different to what you're used to, I suppose.' There was an awkward pause and I took another sip of tea. 'You'll get used to it. It's not bad here.' Another pause. 'It took – Essie a while to settle in. She was homesick for Salzburg, her home town in Austria.'

Essie again, the bestie; was Tasha going to open up now? I was distracted by a commotion on the next table, girls shrieking at something on a smartphone, unaware a teacher was marching towards them. I turned back to Tasha and she'd moved seats next to Suki.

Four
Adam

'Suspended for *two weeks?*' barked Dad, glaring at me angrily. Turning up on the doorstep unexpectedly that Thursday evening, my case in tow and not dressed in school uniform, had given them a nasty shock, and the first thing him and Mom had assumed was: had I walked out or worse, been excluded? Suspension was the next bad thing. 'Jesus, my superiors will hit the roof!' The military paid my school fees.

Mom took the letter from Dad, scanned it, and demanded shakily, 'What did you do, Adam?'

'Nothing!' I flopped, pissed off, onto the sofa. I'd been the fall guy and it was unfair.

'You don't get suspended for nothing, boy!' said Dad. 'It says here you assaulted another lad and you swapped photos of a girl with your pals on social media.'

'I did no such thing and they're not my pals!'

He grunted.

'Dad, can we discuss it later? I wanna jump in the tub.' I pleaded. Dad was dressed in full uniform and glancing at the clock I added, 'Anyway, you're on duty now, aren't you? I'll explain everything tomorrow, honest.'

'Long enough for you to get your story straight?'

He gave me a final scowl, grabbed his jacket, left the room and slammed the front door behind him.

'I'm innocent, Mom,' I told her helplessly.

'You won't fob me off that easily,' she stated in her proper English accent. 'Have your bath and later you can tell me the whole thing from beginning to end.'

Grumbling under my breath, I grabbed my bag and went upstairs, puffing my cheeks out, relieved that at least the hard bit was over. There was no getting my story straight; there was nothing *to* get straight. What I was going to tell Mom and Dad was the truth, the whole truth, and nothing but the truth.

I unlocked my case and chucked what little I'd packed on the bed in a temper, intending to put it away later: my phone, returned to me by the headmaster, Mr Crane, some books and a few clothes to tide me over for the fortnight. Soaking in the tub, all that occupied my mind was how I was going to get Petrov back for the crap he'd landed us both in. He'd also been suspended and Carlton-Greene had been given a week's worth of detention.

Downstairs, Mom had fish and chips waiting on the table. Delicious; in my opinion, the only good thing the UK had on offer was their fish and fries. I was forever being reminded the Brits called them chips and I guessed that was right: they were chipped potatoes. I changed into jogging bottoms and T-shirt and sat down to tuck in.

'Right,' said Mom, pouring out the tea and sitting down opposite, 'let's hear it.'

I was starving, having not eaten since breakfast, merely a boiled egg and toast.

'It was Pictapost.' I began.

Mom bristled. 'Haven't I warned you that Pictapost is dangerous?' she snapped. Mom was a media studies tutor at a local college and lectured on social media a lot. 'It's a hotbed for catfishing...'

'I know, Mom. The thing is I've been really lonely at The Priory. My classmates have got it in for me and Pictapost is – it's all that keeps me going.'

She took a sip of tea.

'Go on.'

'There is – there *was* – a girl.'

'I gathered that from the letter.'

'A guy in my class found out I was contacting her. She posted a picture...'

She waited and I blushed, thinking back to how stupid I'd been for not getting round to reporting the damaged catch on my sports locker, which had been bust for weeks, to the janitor. Gym class over, I'd intended to see if Cherry had responded to my latest

Pictapost message and my phone was wrapped in my clothes at the back of the locker.

'Are you lonely at your new school?' I'd asked. I was very attracted to Cherry and I related to being alone and struggling to fit in; we had that in common and she appeared kind of sad in her photos. I was eager to reach out to her.

I'd removed my key band from my wrist and discovered the door was slightly ajar.

'And my phone had gone,' I finished.

Mom was outraged. 'It was stolen?'

'Petrov, a dude in my class…'

There was no need to explain he was Russian, I think the name spoke for itself.

Mom said, 'He took your phone?'

My mind flashed back to me turning away from the locker to see Petrov, Carlton-Greene and some of the others standing by the showers, laughing at *my* smartphone and at me. I grabbed it off Petrov; he'd already shared Cherry's pic of her posing in her uniform around the school. Seeing red, my fist fell hard against his nose.

'How did you get into my phone and my Pictapost account?' I'd bellowed at him, gripping his arm, his nose streaming blood. He'd banged his head against the tiles. One hand was rubbing the back of his head and the other was cupped over his bleeding nose.

'I can't hear you!' I yelled.

His speech was muffled behind his hand. 'I said I hacked it!'

'You hacked...!'

'You've broken my bloody nose!'

Hearing all the commotion, Jenson came running in, helped to dress Petrov and drove him off to the emergency department at the local hospital. There was no way to escape punishment for hitting him, there'd been too many witnesses, including the prefect carting me off to Crane's office.

'Did you tell Mr Crane all this?'

'In the end,' I confirmed. Everyone at The Priory despised what they called a 'grass'; and yet I owed Petrov. The son of a bitch had ruined my life and I was determined to get my revenge on him somehow. 'I found out later the prefect had already told Crane what had happened, Petrov hacking my phone and...'

'How did he do it?'

'I haven't a clue.' I discovered later that day from Aziz that Petrov was pretty good at breaching computer, tablet and phone security. 'Cherry's picture...'

'Cherry?'

Shit. I hadn't meant to let her name slip out.

'The – the girl on Pictapost whose photo Petrov passed round. I had to tell Crane.'

Mom grimaced. 'You've taken quite a fancy to her, haven't you?'

'Mm, I guess I have.' I pushed my fish around the plate, realising I hadn't eaten very much of it; there was over half left and it was going cold. I dropped my fork. 'I liked her posts and messaged her once. No big deal.'

'How old is she?'

'Sixteen, she says.'

'Show me this photo.'

I was afraid she was going to say that and suddenly, my appetite deserted me.

'OK.'

Fortunately, my Pictapost hadn't been taken down and I'd already saved a screenshot of Cherry's picture. Mom's eyebrows shot up at the raunchy schoolgirl pose and she whistled loudly.

'Attractive girl,' she remarked, 'and foolish for posting that sort of stuff. Serves her right if she's getting all sorts of lewd comments and messages from dirty old men, I bet she's busy deleting them and blocking accounts.' She handed back my phone. 'And you leaving love emojis won't have helped your case,' she added disapprovingly. 'I'm surprised the school allows you to use social media.'

'Why? The school has its own Pictapost account and that's verified and policed.'

'Obviously it is. Tagging the school was a daft thing to do!'

I recalled Crane's words: 'Outrageous, and not the sort of disgusting behaviour we expect from a student at The Priory! I have, of course, removed the tag and reported the matter to the Pictapost moderators.'

'I suppose you shouldn't blame Mr Crane for doing that,' Mom remarked.

'I can blame him for falsely accusing me!'

I'd raged at Crane: 'They'll ban me!'

'Probably.' Crane had sat back comfortably in his chair. 'It's no more than you deserve.'

'I did not tag her!'

'It came from your account.'

Damn that Petrov! I'd lost my Pictapost profile and Cherry forever!

'You're accusing Petrov of hacking into your phone and tagging the photo?' said Crane.

'Yes, I am.'

'I'll investigate that. For now, please go back to your class. Wait,' he held out his hand, 'I'll have that, please.'

I gripped my cell tightly. 'What? Why?'

'I forbid you to contact this girl again,' he said. 'Besides, it's likely your account will be taken down.'

I swore inwardly and dropped the phone on the desk.

Back in the present, Mom said, 'And did he question this lad?'

'He did and Petrov denied it. Crane didn't believe him. I guess he knows Petrov's got form for hacking, that's why Petrov has also been sent home.'

'If Mr Crane knows this Petrov tagged her photo from your account, why have you been suspended?'

'Second strike, Mom; there was that fight in the first semester, remember.'

'A two week suspension for this is a bit harsh.' Mom picked up her own cell phone. 'I think I ought to call Mr Crane, see if I can get this straightened out.'

No chance, Mom.

Within a fortnight of being at the school I'd been in a fight and had been warned not to put a foot wrong again. Now I had and it was second strike.

Mom and Crane had a ten minute animated conversation where her voice increased a few octaves and I heard the words 'bullying' and 'intimidation'. I placed a bowl over the fish and chips and put the plate in the fridge, intending to warm it in the microwave and finish it later. In the lounge, I turned on the TV and flicked around the channels to find an interesting and distracting programme to take my mind off things.

Eventually, Mom joined me and said flatly, 'He's confirmed it, saying you've been suspended for giving the school a bad name; however, he accepts that was down to this other lad.'

Told ya.

'Third strike,' Mom continued, chucking her phone on the coffee table in irritation, 'and you're out.'

I wish.

'You mentioned bullying,' I said.

Mom collapsed on the couch next to me, grabbed the TV remote and switched off the set.

'That's what I'd call it and he said he'd look into it,' she said, 'and I'll remind him. Please behave at The Priory, Adam. Promise me you'll try and settle in and at least stick it out till the end of this year.'

I winced, having heard this speech a million times in the past. Grandpa had been an English teacher at The Priory and had died of cancer at the young age of thirty-six, therefore, Mom expected me to live up to his memory by being a model student there. The difference was, Grandpa had been a Brit and used to the establishment, whereas I was from the States, and England's dumb stiff upper lip, rugby, soccer and cricket, was an alien world to me. My parents assumed I'd settled in there and had no clue how bad the bullying got. Should I speak out now?

'Mom, I...'

'I appreciate how hard you're finding it, love,' she interrupted, 'and if you're struggling by the end of the year I promise we'll discuss sending you elsewhere. The thing is, you've moved around that often and it's been unsettling for you. I was hoping you'd see out your schooldays there and leave at eighteen.'

Three long years away!

'And you have important exams coming up.' She paused. 'You won't get a good job unless you pass them. It's up to you if you go to university or get a job in the military. Think on that without good exam results you won't get far in this world.'

It was pointless arguing that I was innocent and I was being picked on for being American.

'I hear you, Mom. I promise to behave from now on.'

If my classmates leave me alone.

She patted my hand. 'Cheer up, love. Dad will be home tomorrow and we can talk again. He'll be keen to hear the whole story and he won't be happy either way. Forget it for now. You've got a fortnight off and there'll be plenty for you to do to help around here, on top of the schoolwork and Zoom lessons they're giving you.'

'Great,' I mumbled.

Although she was obviously disappointed in me, Mom was actually reasonable and calm, simply one of those things, she said, and I had to learn from it. On the other hand, Dad went to the other extreme and off the scale. He ranted, raved and slammed things, breaking the fruit dish and earning a tirade from Mom to prevent him from causing damage to anything else. He directed most of his anger towards Crane and Petrov, calling him all the anti-Russian names under the sun.

'Adam isn't entirely in the wrong, honey,' he said to Mom. 'Hell, it's healthy and natural for a boy to drool over a girl and is certainly not a crime. All he needs is to keep his nose clean from now on and get his grades.'

'You gotta sort out that attitude of yours, boy,' he said to me later, sweeping up the broken dish pieces and covering them in bubble wrap before placing them in a trash bag. 'You gotta learn to live at that school and step up. Your Mom is right: education is important and The Priory is a fine establishment, one of the elites in this country, even if it isn't a military school.'

He'd gone to an ordinary high school in New Jersey and done well, beginning at basic airman level and working his way up to captain during his ten years there. The air force was his life and he was enthusiastic for me to join up one day. Sadly for him, the military wasn't in my blood.

'*You* want me to be educated in the States,' I reminded him angrily. 'The military can easily pay for me to go to a boarding-school there. Why do I have to stay in the UK and be stuck in some posh limey hellhole? And why isn't the school down the road good enough?'

'The only place in the US good enough for you is a military school and your mom won't hear of it,' he retorted. 'She insisted on The Priory and that's all there is to it. Quit griping, Adam! You've had a better start than I had. Now drop it and don't mess up the one chance you have of succeeding in life. You owe it to yourself and to your mom.'

There was obviously nothing more to be said.

Five
Cherry

Things were on the up.

Rahma and Suki were a lot more approachable and Tasha was thawing a bit. On the home front, however, it was a different story. I began to hear less and less from Precious and Suze. They were in no rush to reply to my messages, giving me little choice but to focus on potential friendships at Helton. I was grateful for Tulip's regular calls and messages, always reminding me she was there for me if I needed her. I dreaded meeting Precious and Suze again in the holidays and that added more fuel to my hatred of Greg; he'd ruined my life, turned it upside down.

I made a massive effort to win over my roommates and clung to my new online relationship, getting a shock when, alone in the study bedroom one Saturday afternoon trying to catch up on extra Maths prep, I found out Adam had tagged my sexy schoolgirl pose to everyone on his list, including his school's account! I was surprised The Priory was on Pictapost, considering Helton's opinion on social media.

'What the...?' I said out loud at the comments and direct messages. How could he do such a thing! There was a message from a John Crane, headmaster at The Priory School, apologising for the behaviour of one of his pupils and that the Pictapost moderators had been notified. I was advised to block the offender immediately.

'WTF, Adam!' I tapped furiously. 'You've tagged my pic to your whole list!'

Not hearing from him right away infuriated me and cramming on Maths went right out of the window. I abandoned my books and took angry selfies of me lying on my bed, my phone pinging non-stop: 'Hello, gorgeous, can I give you my number?' and 'Take another pic without your bra on!' amongst other disgusting remarks. Then I caught a glimpse of a message that flashed up from an account called @ceridwen_: 'I'm really sorry your photo was tagged. Please be careful.'

Where they being nice or just plain creepy?

Suki, staggering through the door, dressed in her hockey gear, mud on her cheek, arms, legs and boots, carrying her stick and weighed down by her sports bag, brought me back from my virtual world. She was in the first hockey team and was supposed to shower and change in the sports pavilion, a strict rule. I was surprised to see her in this state, leaving a trail of mud behind her.

'How did you get in without being seen?' I enquired curiously, forgetting the photo for a moment. 'There's mud everywhere!'

She tapped her nose. 'I have my methods. Give us a hand, will you, darling?'

I jumped up and grabbed the bag from her.

'Jesus, Suki, what have you got in here?' I dumped it on her bed and heard the distinct clinking of bottles.

'Oooh, be careful!'

Dropping her stick to the floor, she unzipped the bag, revealing a change of clothes and, hidden underneath, a couple of boxes of chocolates, four packs of multi-bag crisps, two bottles of lemonade, two bottles of white wine and one bottle of Bacardi rum.

'Suki! Where did you get all this stuff?'

'Help me hide it and I'll tell you.'

Rapidly, we stashed it in the back of her wardrobe and she collapsed on her bed, proceeding to take off her muddy boots and change into her jogging bottoms and top.

'Oh, I suppose I'd better clean up the crap I've left outside in case Carter notices it,' she said.

Fortunately, the broom and dust pan we found in the domestics' cupboard on our landing effectively cleared the dirt. We also swept the carpet outside our room and on the stairs, and intended to go down to the main hall to tidy up there, if we hadn't been disturbed by our house mother's exasperated voice drifting up the stairs.

'Where did this all this mud come from? Has somebody come in from the playing field without changing?'

'Bloody hell!' hissed Suki and we ran, giggling, into our room, being careful not to slam the door.

'You'd better hide your kit and your boots,' I advised. 'If Carter walks in and sees it...'

'I'll take everything into the shower, wash them in there!' Suki chuckled. 'I'll bring them back in my sports bag. They'll dry on the radiator.'

'They'll drip all over the floor!' I flopped down on my bed. 'Now, come on, Suki, tell me where you got this lot and why.'

'I had it delivered,' Suki informed me, stuffing her dirty kit and hockey boots into her sports bag, 'from the supermarket in the town. Erm, a lad working there dropped it off for me at the bus-stop.'

'Oh, yeah?' was all I said. The young men in the town swarmed around her and she'd been warned on more than one occasion to keep away from them.

Suki winked. 'It's Tasha-chan's birthday next Friday and we're going to have a party. That girl desperately needs cheering up. I'm sick and tired of her moping around the place every day!'

'A party? I didn't realise Tasha was the partying type. Where are we having it?'

'In here. On Friday night, of course, and on the Saturday we can nurse our hangovers! Not that we're going to drink the booze straight, the lemonade will water it down.'

I laughed. 'That doesn't mean we won't get hammered! How are we going to fit everyone in here?'

'We're not. It'll be the four of us. Tasha doesn't really mix with the other girls in our class. Not a word to her, mind.' Suki grabbed her towel, toiletry bag and sports bag and opened the door. 'It has to be a surprise.'

Would Tasha agree to a party and allow the drink to let her open up to me about Essie?

Suki left for her shower. My phone pinged again and brought my mind back to the problem of the tagged picture. A message from Adam at last:

'I'm innocent, Cherry, I swear! My account was hacked by a classmate.'

'Why?'

'He did it for a joke, I guess. We've both been suspended. I hit him and it served him right! My account will probably be deleted. I guess you'd better block me.'

I paused. Blocking him was the right thing to do, the sensible thing to do. Walk away. I was angry and not entirely certain I believed his story; the problem was I really liked him. We had things in common, trying to settle in at a new school and fitting in.

'Not a bad idea,' I agreed, and abruptly ended the conversation.

I almost went further and deleted my entire account, deciding to switch to private instead, to dodge any further rude comments and risks of further tagging from anyone on my list to the outside world. Some of my old posts had been tagged, not by Adam, and I removed the tags and blocked the accounts. If my account was private, people had to request to connect and I'd return the favour, if I chose to.

Another comment from @ceridwen_: 'I've been through what you're going through now. Some people aren't what they seem. Watch your step. It'll end badly.'

Who's this?

I studied the profile: it was blank, no avatar pic, no posts, no friend list and one person on their follow list: me. I was intrigued. Was it a new account and had it been stalking my posts?

Suki returned from the shower and Ceridwen still hadn't got back to me, so I tried to forget it.

Unable to bring myself to block Adam, I decided to ghost him, not prepared to see if I had messages and if his account remained active. On the Monday, curiosity finally got the better of me and there were no notifications. I searched for his account name: @adamfishofficial had gone from our conversations. I was surprised by how upset I was. We'd formed a bond, now he was gone.

On Friday night, I was ready for Tasha's party and to let my hair down. Abiding by tradition, the class sang *Happy Birthday* to her at breakfast and each girl gave her a gift.

'Thanks, everyone,' said Tasha shyly, blushing and clearly uncomfortable by all the attention. Rahma had bought her a lovely silver compact mirror, Suki a bath and shower gel set and I got her a set of four perfumed colourful Yankee candles, her favourites. Of course, Clarissa Cleverly had to show off and produced the most expensive present of all, a bottle of Chanel No 5. In return, it was traditional to share a birthday cake at tea and Tasha's mum had ordered a fantastic one from Harrods, red roses adorning the edge of the white icing and *Happy Birthday Tasha* was piped in red lettering on the top. It was big enough for everyone to have a good-sized piece and tasted yummy.

'It's not right you have to be in school today, Tash,' said Suki, putting her arm through Tasha's and leading her into class. 'Anyone whose birthday falls on a school day should automatically have that day off.'

'That's not fair on those of us who have birthdays in July!' Rahma said, poking her in the ribs. Suki's birthday was in October and mine in May.

School, tea and prep over, we had the evening to ourselves and Tasha was in a good mood, laughing and cracking jokes on our way up to our room to change out of uniform.

'Who's up for a swim?' she said.

The indoor pool was used all year round, closing at eight in the evening, popular in winter, in cold, wet weather; it had been showery and windy all day. We spent a happy hour splashing around and joining in an impromptu game of water polo with some other girls.

On Fridays, our class was allowed to go to bed at ten-thirty and Tasha suggested joining in the rave in the gym, starting at eight and ending at ten. A brother of a girl in the Sixth Form was a DJ and had been booked to do the music. Suki shook her head.

'Nah, I'm not in the mood to be sociable tonight,' she said, stretching and feigning weariness. 'It's been a tough week.'

'All right, what shall we do?' said Tasha. 'Everyone else is going and what if we're missed?'

'I was thinking...' began Rahma.

'And me...' I joined in.

Tasha put her hand on our bedroom door handle to open it. 'Thinking what?'

'Ah...' said Suki and Rahma's hands went over her eyes.

'Hey! What's going on?' cried Tasha in shock. I helped Suki lead her into the room, all four of us laughing. 'What are you up to?' You haven't got me a stripper-gram, have you?'

'No, the next best thing!' I said. 'Mr Ross is coming to give you a lap dance!'

Shrieks of mirth and protest; Mr Ross, the music teacher, was seventy if he was a day.

'Oh, come on!' begged Tasha. 'I'll burst if you don't tell me what's going on!'

'In a moment, darling!' Suki dragged the bottles, chocolates and crisps out of the bottom of her wardrobe. 'Right, Rahma-chan, we're ready!'

Rahma removed her hands and Tasha blinked at the bunting draped over her bed headboard, the colourful balloons on her pillows and the food and booze on her dressing-table.

'What's all this?' she gasped, bending down and grabbing a bottle. 'Oh, WOW! Bacardi! You naughty girls!'

'Surprise!' we chorused.

'Part-aaaaaaaaaaay!' cried Suki.

'For me?'

'Of course for you, you daft thing!' Rahma laughed. 'What do you think, Tash? Are you up for a pyjama party?'

'Yeah, not half!' Tasha nodded enthusiastically. 'Only what if a teacher walks in? It's a pity we can't lock the door.'

Bedroom doors were also fire doors and it was a strict rule not to lock them on the inside. Many girls grumbled that this went against their privacy and human rights, in spite of no one daring to disobey it.

'Most of the teachers will be at the rave,' said Rahma, dropping her jogging bottoms and proceeding to get into her silk pyjamas. 'Mind you, I suppose if we are missed one of them might come round on the prowl.'

Suki suppressed a yawn. 'I'm having a glass of wine now,' she stated. 'We can stash the stuff back in the wardrobe and if we hear footsteps it won't take us long to hide this lot.'

'You haven't invited anyone else, have you?' enquired Tasha worriedly. 'That *will* bring the wolves to the door if we have a whole mob squashed in here!'

'Nah, they weren't invited,' I assured her, taking down our coffee mugs from the bookshelf. 'The others are at the rave. This is *our* party!'

Ten minutes later, we were in our pyjamas and dressing-gowns, swigging merlot and finding everything hilarious, my woes over Adam forgotten. At around eight, the low thumping base from the gym reached our ears. The rave was underway.

'Shush!' I urged. 'The wolves!'

Tasha hiccupped. 'Which one of the staff reminds you of a wolf more than any other?'

On strips of paper from a page I tore out of my English exercise book, we wrote down the names of five staff each we decided closely resembled a wolf, and dropped them into Tasha's bobble hat.

'Who's…' I burped and examined my mug. I'd have to slow down otherwise I'd be legless soon. '…gonna count the votes? OO-ER!' I belched again. 'I think I'm wellied already!'

Suki crawled to the wardrobe and brought out a bottle of lemonade.

'Pass me your mugs,' she slurred, opening the bottle. 'I forgot to add this to the drinks to water them down. We'll get smashed too soon and be fast asleep by nine-thirty. WOW!' She guffawed, realising it had fizzed over her pyjama bottoms. 'I've wet my pants!'

We all helped ourselves to a generous amount of lemonade while she changed into another pair of PJs.

'I'll do the counting,' said Rahma, putting down her mug and taking up Tasha's hat.

Carefully, she took out the strips of paper. The result was unanimous.

'And the winner is...'

'Mrs Sharma!' we chorused in delight.

'No surprise there, the horrible old bitch!' I raised my mug in salute.

'Hush!' gurgled the others.

'What's that din?' said Rahma suddenly, knowing perfectly well it was the fire alarm.

'Oh, you are kidding me!' groaned Suki. 'Is the toast burning again?'

That was one reason why toasters, kettles and irons had been banned from study bedrooms: any smoke alarms going off in one building triggered the alarms all over the school, the fire brigade turned up and the girls whistled and catcalled at the male crew. Kettles were allowed in the common-rooms, otherwise we had to use the kitchen to make toast and iron our clothes.

'Can anyone smell burning?' I said, sniffing the air. The music from the gym had stopped and girls were pouring out to the courtyard.

'It'll be a false alarm, surely,' said Suki, visibly annoyed at the disruption. 'Let's pretend we haven't heard it.'

'Better not.' Rahma hiccupped. 'They'll come round and inspect the rooms. Come on,' she staggered to her feet, 'better get our coats on.'

'What the – it's chucking it down out!' cried Tasha, indicating the rain lashing against the window.

'Yeah; doesn't it always pee down during a fire drill?' said Rahma, rolling her eyes.

Reluctantly, we hastily stored our mugs, wine and lemonade bottles under Suki's bed, arranged Tasha's duvet over her decorations and grabbed our coats.

All of a sudden, the clanging ceased.

'Uh?' said Suki.

Our door opened and one of the prefects popped her head in.

'Oh, you *are* here,' she said. We all tried to look innocent. 'All sorted. The DJ's music deck tripped the electricity and cut the power off. Why aren't you in the gym; you're missing a great party!' She frowned at us. 'Bit early to be in your jimjams, isn't it? What's going on?'

It was a horrible moment and we were temporarily robbed of speech. A girl behind her said, 'There you are, Marilyn! Let's go, the party's on again.'

'Coming!'

She closed the door and we flopped on our beds.

'That was a close one!' said Tasha, taking off her coat.

'I've got a brill idea how to keep people out without locking the door,' Suki declared, and that was to shove my chest-of-drawers against it.

That deed done, she added, 'More wine and lemonade, anyone?' and assembled the bottles back on her dressing-table.

'I think we'll keep the rum for another day,' said Rahma, guzzling two-thirds wine to one-third lemonade. 'Urgh-k! That's sharp!'

I puffed out my cheeks, fearing I was going to throw up. 'I think I've had enough to drink!'

'Lightweight!' remarked Suki, filling her mug up again.

'You are a bit green around the gills,' agreed Tasha sympathetically. 'Stick to lemonade from now on.'

'No, thanks, I've had enough.' I put my half-finished wine on top of my bedside table and snuggled down under my duvet.

Rahma said woozily, 'Anyone fancy a game of Twister?'

'Yeah!'

Out came the box from under Rahma's bed and she spread the mat out on the floor.

'Come on, Cherry-chan,' coaxed Suki.

'Leave her,' advised Rahma. 'She's almost spark out!'

I heard giggling and Suki calling me a lightweight again. Smiling, I peeped at them and saw three bodies, arms and legs, twisted on the mat and there was much hilarity. It was nice to see Tasha enjoying her party. I was safer lying down. Inhaling deeply, I tried to swallow down the nausea to prevent emptying the contents of my stomach on the carpet!

My phone buzzed in my dressing-gown pocket and I took it out. It was a notification from Pictapost; a request from someone called Danny, and one word: 'Hello.'

I gaped at it for a moment before tapping the avatar pic and scrutinising the account. There were six photos, selfies of a dark-haired guy, his intense, almost unreal brown eyes, so dark they were enticing.

'Nice,' I said aloud.

Suki, using her hand as a fan and laughing, flopped down next to me.

'What's nice?'

I showed her and she nodded her approval. She took the phone from me and flicked through his photos.

'Mm mm *mm!*' she exclaimed. 'Hey, Rahma, Tasha, come and see this hot bloke Cherry's found!'

They scrambled away from the Twister mat and surrounded Suki. Moving onto my back, I focused dreamily at the ceiling. Suki tapped at my phone screen and Rahma laughed and clapped.

'Suki!' I cried, laughing and trying to grab the phone off her. 'Oh, you wait!'

'Hello, Danny ❤!' she'd written, and tapped *Accept*. 'There you go!' she said triumphantly. 'You can thank me at your wedding! Bags me chief bridesmaid!'

'You daft cow!' I said affectionately, half-aware of Tasha sitting back on her heels, clutching her mug of wine, staring blankly at us.

The message request landed in my inbox from Ceridwen the next morning.

Six
Adam

A promise was a promise and I didn't want to hurt my mom by refusing to return to The Priory. On Zoom my teachers guided me through the work I was missing and set me exercises I had to complete and return via email for marking. Four hours of homework every day kept me busy. I guessed Petrov was suffering the same fate. Once school was done for the day, Dad had me doing odd jobs, gardening and helping him in the garage.

As expected, my Pictapost account had been shut down and that left me empty and alone in the world. Cherry had set her account to private, meaning if I got set up again using a different email address and login I wouldn't see her posts, apart from her avatar pic. Not enough. Sending a friend request was probably pointless if she no longer trusted me. Searching her profile through Google Images to get photos that way was fruitless and left me bereft. I couldn't find her on any other social media sites like Twitter, Facebook, Instagram and TikTok, unless she used different names on those.

All that, and the resentment I continued to harbour against Petrov, increased my desire of revenge on him. I'd always intended to get back at him somehow for the wrong he'd done and what I considered to be the perfect idea sprouting in my mind began to be mapped out.

I did a lot of thinking that fortnight on the base. I'd survive at The Priory if I had buddies on my side. The problem was, everyone thought I was a grass, but I had to fit in somehow and craved acceptance and trust from people, especially Daniil Petrov.

Uncomfortably, we arrived back at school within minutes of one another, Petrov in a large, impressive, black chauffeur-driven limo, accompanied by a woman I presumed was his mom, and me alone in a taxi, having travelled by train. The taxi driver got my case and rucksack out of the trunk and the chauffeur handed Petrov a large navy blue hold-all. Petrov spoke to the woman and they both frowned at me. She sneered and got back into the car. The chauffeur shut the door, got into the driver's seat and drove off. I dragged my case behind me and walked towards him.

'Nice car,' I remarked pleasantly.

'Thanks,' he said, turning away towards the school entrance.

'Is it a Senat?'

He directed his strange, magnetic glare at me. 'Yes. Do you know much about cars?'

'A bit; my dad's pal is a car dealer in the States.'

'I see.'

One of the teachers came out to welcome us and that brought our very short conversation to an abrupt end.

Having missed supper, we were given tea and sandwiches in the common-room, where the others welcomed Petrov back with fist pumps and hugs all round. All I got from Carlton-Greene was, 'Hello, grass.'

I inhaled a deep, silent breath, trying not to betray any hint of anger.

Aziz said, 'Lay off, CG, Fisher's no grass, Forrester told Crane what happened.'

Forrester was the prefect who'd witnessed the fight and taken me to see Crane. Carlton-Greene sniffed and slouched off.

Aziz turned to me. 'Good to see you back, mate.' He held out his hand and I took it gratefully, ignoring Petrov and the others' stupid, jokey, wolf-whistling noises.

'Bang to rights, Petrov!' Aziz teased. 'How about an apology to end all this aggro?'

Petrov, illegally vaping, blew out a puff of smoke. 'Good idea. He hasn't apologised to me.'

'Not Fisher; you, you tool!'

'Me?'

'You hacked Fisher's phone and sent the pic of that girl round to everyone, including me. No wonder he punched you; it's no more than you deserved.'

Petrov scowled at Aziz in silence and another guy said, 'He's right, Petrov. It was a rotten thing you did, stealing Fisher's phone and hacking into it.'

Murmurs of agreement at this statement and Petrov pursed his lips.

'Come on, Petrov,' insisted Aziz, 'what you did was out of order and you've got previous for doing this sort of thing. I haven't forgotten what you did to my tablet.'

'*What* did I do to your tablet?' demanded Petrov, clearly flustered by Aziz's remark.

'Hacked into it and signed me up to a porn site! Boobs all over my screen, there were!'

Roars of laughter greeted this. Petrov's mouth twitched and I snorted.

'Lucky for you I have a sense of humour,' said Aziz, chuckling. 'Eh, Petrov? You apologised to me – eventually.'

'Yeah, you'd better say you're sorry, Petrov,' piped up Carlton-Greene, 'otherwise, you won't hear the end of it, and to be fair, you did mess up. You got caught, for one thing!'

Petrov sniffed, muttered something inaudible, turned to me and mumbled, 'Sorry.'

I put my hand to my ear. 'What? I missed that.'

'SORRY!'

Aziz said, 'He doesn't mean it, Fisher, you can tell. I think it's the best you're gonna get, though.'

'Yeah.'

There was no point pushing it any further. Petrov sulked for the rest of that evening and most of the next day. Aziz brushed it off. He handled Petrov no problem and they always ended up on speaking terms again.

We unpacked our bags, ate our sandwiches and obeyed the summons from Crane's office. Petrov was interviewed first and I sat in the waiting-room. Ten minutes later, I saw him marching along the corridor through the glass-panelled wall and depart through the swing doors leading to the exit. Crane's secretary arrived shortly afterwards.

'Your turn to go in, Fisher.'

Crane's office door was on the other side of her desk. I knocked and was told to enter.

'Ah, Fisher,' said Crane. 'Take a seat. How was your fortnight?'

I shrugged, recognising Petrov's vaporiser lying on the shelf behind him. He must have been spotted using it and had had it confiscated.

'You managed the Zoom lessons all right?'

'Yes.'

'Good. In that case, you won't have a lot to catch up on back in class.'

'No.'

'And your Pictapost account has gone, I see.'

I hesitated, trying not to show any resentment. 'Yes.'

'It's for the best. Thank you, Mary.' The secretary came in and placed a cup of coffee and a plate of four cookies in front of him. He took a sip of the coffee, replaced the cup on its saucer and added, 'Of course, there's nothing I can do to prevent you from setting up another. Have you?'

That brought me up short. 'Have I what?'

'Set up another Pictapost account.'

'No.'

I won't tell you if I do.

'Get set up again,' Scott had begged me on a Zoom call. 'Ignore that Crane guy.'

'Will you?' said Crane now.

'I haven't decided.'

'If you do, ensure it's private, keep your interests harmless and your phone away from Petrov, and stop contacting impressionable young girls constantly exposing themselves and showing off everything they've got. It's how they get drawn in by online predators. I suspect she gets quite a lot of unsavoury attention, posting revealing photos. I've warned my daughters to be careful on social media.'

Yeah, I bet you have. Crane and his wife – also our Head of Modern Languages – lived in a private house on the outskirts of the town. Their fifteen- and seventeen-year-old daughters attended a local private day school and were worth looking at from what I'd heard. They weren't allowed anywhere near The Priory school building.

'That Cherry is a stupid girl,' Crane rattled on, 'and what were you thinking, losing your head over her! Online flirting is a dangerous game. Petrov has form for hacking and that's why I suspended him. You were suspended for violence and remember, Fisher, you're on a final warning and I've told Petrov his behaviour is being closely monitored. He's been skating on thin ice these past months.'

And you have no intention of excluding him, have you? Whose rich oligarch daddy paid for the new swimming pool and sports pavilion?

I shifted uncomfortably in my seat, wishing he'd shut up and let me leave.

'You've eaten?'

'Yes, sandwiches in the common-room.'

'Good.' Crane waved me away. 'You may go, and if I hear any more negative accounts of your behaviour from now on, you're out.'

Back in the common-room, a few people were glued to a late kick-off ball game on TV, and since the rules of soccer/football/whatever-they-called-it in this damp, depressing country went over my head, I spent the time listening to music on my phone wearing my headphones and surfing social media, noting impatiently that Cherry's Pictapost was still set to private. It was frustrating she had no other accounts. Crane's question rang in my ears, '*Have you set up another Pictapost account?*' and my heart thumped.

Petrov was absent from the common-room. Either he'd gone to bed early or sneaked out to the town to get another vaporiser, a risk that was bound to get him into deep trouble if he was caught.

I found his Pictapost account, a private one, subtly named: @_p_e_t_r_o_v_. Petrov's avatar was a selfie, clean-shaven, slightly younger than now, his strange, intense dark gaze drawing me in and it was hard not to appreciate his photos. I imagined Dean falling head over heels in love.

A scream of 'GOAL!' brought me out of my daydream. Aziz, preferring cricket to soccer and concentrating on a book instead of the match, now came over and sat next to me.

'Hi,' he said. 'Glad to be back?'

'I guess.'

'You won't feel like an outsider forever, you'll settle down. The Priory is a good school.'

'I'm not an outsider,' I retorted defensively. 'I'm a white American and Petrov is Russian. He's more of an outsider than I am. The Brits hate the Russians, right?'

I could have bitten my tongue. Why did I say that? The last thing on my mind was to offend Aziz.

He laughed. 'No, I'm not white, nor are the Falade brothers, nor any of the other black and Asian lads in this school; however, the Russians and the other Eastern Europeans are charmers and can easily win people over. Petrov oozes charm and it's hard not to respect that.'

'Even if he did mess up your tablet and sign you up for a porn site?' I said slyly.

His shy, dreamy expression got me thinking. Little things came to mind: Aziz standing suggestively close to Petrov, displaying little hints of affection, the light touches on Petrov's back, on his arms and shoulders, and the long, greeting hugs. Did Aziz have the hots for Petrov? Not that I had a problem if he did; my amazement was more Petrov being his choice. I had other gay pals apart from Dean in the States and quite a few people at The Priory were out. Was I searching for signs in Aziz that weren't there?

His hand went on my knee and I nearly jumped out of my skin.

'Petrov's a great lad really. Why not try to get along? He has many great qualities.'

I said nothing. Aziz removed his hand, winked and went back to his chair. Gulping, I waited for my pulse to slow down and slipped out of the common-room at the first opportunity.

I decided to go up to the dorm for an early night. I was exhausted,: it had been a long, dreary train journey from the base thanks to constant hold-ups on the rail track and I was a bit depressed at being back, preferring to wallow in self-pity. I was surprised to see Petrov – he slept in the dorm next door – lounging on Carlton-Greene's bed, swiping his phone and vaping, smoke rising in the air.

'Hello,' I said casually. He raised his hand without glancing up. 'What are you doing here?'

'Vaping, of course.'

'I can see that.' It smelled strongly of strawberry. 'How many vapes do you have? I saw one on Crane's desk.'

Petrov directed those amazing, steely eyes of his towards me. 'I don't at the moment. That was my last one. Freddie has a few of these stashed away; he said to take one until I'm able to buy more. We have a secret hiding place for them, away from Crane and the prefect police.'

There were regular spot-checks for cigarettes, vapes, drugs and booze.

I collapsed on my bed and started to unlace my sneakers. Petrov took a long puff and offered the vape to me.

'No, thanks.'

'Go on,' he coaxed. 'Try it. It'll loosen you up a bit.'

'Am I that uptight?'

He was being unusually pleasant and naturally I was cautious; nevertheless, I accepted the invitation and took a puff.

'It doesn't taste of anything much,' I remarked. 'What's the appeal? To look cool?'

'No.' He snatched the vape back. 'It gives me the same kick a cigarette does, without the same quantity of nicotine. It's the next best thing without the real deal. Have you ever smoked?'

'No.'

'Do you have any vices?'

'Sure.' I wasn't going to tell him what they were.

He put the vape and his phone in his pocket.

'I'm off back to the common-room. Coming?' He noticed me grab my pyjamas from under my pillow. 'Uh? Going to bed *already?* At twenty-past eight?'

'It's been a long day. I'm tired and they have a soccer match on the TV.'

'Oh, of course, you won't be interested in that. You Americans don't do real football, do you?'

'It's more of a woman's sport in the US.'

I began to unbutton my shirt, then, mindful of Aziz's possible attraction for Petrov, I speculated whether he shared those feelings, and became suddenly unnerved by his stare, left my shirt alone, and turned my attention to my phone.

He took the hint and stood up. 'Goodnight.'

'Yeah, same to you.'

I watched him walk out of the dorm and close the door. Frustratingly, sleep escaped me, not helped by the laughter and voices echoing around the building. Sighing, I unlocked my bedside drawer and prepared putting my plan into action.

Now for Petrov to pay for his sins.

Seven
Cherry

I was on cloud nine.

Danny was from Los Angeles in the USA, aged nineteen, worked in a bank and contacted me virtually every hour, on the hour, making written love to me and telling me how beautiful I was. It was music to my ears and what I needed in my lonely world, a sophisticated older man taking an interest in me. Both Mum and Tulip remained my lifeline at home; Rahma, Suki and Tasha were becoming my school family, mainly due to our little party for Tasha's birthday. We were getting closer, except I needed more in my life, and that was Danny. I was head over heels; he'd awoken feelings in me that alarmed and thrilled me, and was successful in taking my mind off Adam. Where was Adam? What was he doing? Did I care?

Not any more.

Danny was the real thing for me and I daydreamed that one day we'd meet up. A lot of couples met on social media and Suki had joined Tinder to get random dates whenever she stayed in London; both Rahma and Tasha disapproved. I fretted if Danny went quiet. Often he said it was because of his diabetes and he sent me photos of the insulin he had to take. I was sorry he had to go through that every day. It was silly how I'd fallen for a boy I hadn't met and how a random photograph sent my spirits into overdrive. I ached for him at every waking moment and his words and pictures caused my body to tingle. I was convinced it was love, real love, and I craved every second of his online attention.

One thing marred it and that was Ceridwen.

At first, I hadn't minded what seemed to be genuine concern by this stranger (it had to be a female: on Googling the name I'd discovered Ceridwen was a Welsh enchantress, a witch, in fact); but she was a real pain in the arse. Blocking the account was fruitless: @Cerid.wen, @Ceri.dwen and other variants of the name popped up, leaving messages and comments on Danny's posts: 'Fake!' 'Scammer!' 'Catfish!' and on mine: 'Block him! He's leading you up the garden path and he's no good!'

It was all really unsettling. Danny said, 'Ignore it. It's a crank.'

That was easier said than done. I deleted the comments and the direct messages without reading them. It nearly persuaded me to shut down my account altogether and set up a new one. Nah; why do that? I had to keep reporting this nutcase, hoping she'd take the hint and do one.

Rahma and Suki were always teasing me about Danny, during break, at meals and in our room; they longed to see if he'd messaged again. Tasha, on the other hand, showed no interest whatsoever.

'Oh, Cherry-chan! He's gorgeous!' cried Suki, adoringly ogling the latest pic of him in a crisp, white T-shirt, the word *Hot* emblazoned in capitals on the front in black capital letters. She'd sent him a request and despite inviting him to chat, he hadn't engaged.

'I'm clearly not his type,' she'd observed in mock-gloom. I laughed. Suki had no room for any more admirers. Her life and her social media was already chock full of them and Danny was mine, not hers.

'Now, Suki, Cherry saw him first,' Rahma pointed out, grinning and patting her hand consolingly. 'He's dreamy and clearly fancies you, Cherry. I hate you!' she added good-naturedly.

I waited in vain for Tasha's opinion. Suki said, 'I bet he'd love to meet you.'

'He's said so,' I said bashfully.

Unexpectedly, Tasha blurted, 'I wouldn't get your hopes up on that score, Cherry. That'll be him feeding you false promises he'll have no intention of living up to.'

'What's your problem, Tash?' I said irritably. 'It's a bit of fun and anyway, meeting up hasn't been discussed. We've not been in contact for that long.'

'Has he asked for your phone number?' she enquired. I caught Rahma and Suki exchanging a sly glance and wondered what it meant.

'No. Not yet.'

My emotions raced. What if he did? Was I ready to take that step in our relationship?

'Don't let him force you into giving it to him,' she warned.

'Shush!' hissed Suki, nudging her. The teacher had entered the room and we had to end the conversation.

I was puzzled. Why *was* Tasha so preoccupied with Danny and me? She wouldn't say. If I tried to broach the subject, either she clammed up or walked away. I was getting edgy, turning to Suki and Rahma for information. One weekend, Tasha had gone home to see her family and me, Suki and Rahma were in our room getting ready for bed.

'Can either of *you* tell me why Tasha is dead set against me messaging Danny on Pictapost?'

'No, not really,' replied Rahma cagily. Suki spun round and chucked her hairbrush on the bed.

'Oh, come on, Rahma-chan, darling, she can hear the story. What harm can it do? Everyone else in the Manor knows chapter and verse.'

Rahma rubbed hand cream around her palms and said nothing. I was agitated. What story? Rahma finished moisturising her hands, pulled back her duvet cover and climbed into bed.

'Suki's referring to Essie,' she said.

'Essie?'

Suki nodded and finished undressing. Was I going to discover the mystery behind Essie's demise at long last?

'Yeah; in Year Ten, Essie met a dude on Pictapost,' Suki explained, shimmying elegantly into her nightie and grabbing her lady shave from her dressing-table. 'He said he was a car salesman from Texas in America and of course he was an awful lot older, at least he was in the photos he sent Essie.'

'He told her he was thirty-one,' added Rahma.

'Thirty-one?' Without knowing why, I shivered. 'What happened?'

'Tasha and Essie were best mates from day one in Year Seven,' said Suki, running the lady shave over her shins. 'Essie messaged him a lot – he said his name was Cody – and became obsessed. Essie had been really fun, such a lovely person and really fond of Tasha. It was really sad how that man changed her.' She paused to pick up her buzzing phone, swiped the screen and giggled; probably a text from one of her many male fans.

'Essie changed overnight,' Rahma took up the tale. 'She became a wreck, waking us up by pacing up and down the room and letting herself go, gave up sleeping, eating, washing and brushing her hair altogether, and lost a lot of weight. No one had a clue what was wrong, not even Tasha, and it stressed us all out.'

'The pair of them sent us up the wall,' continued Suki. 'Tasha was forever crying over it and Essie collapsed in class one day and ended up in the san. They called the doctor and he said it was some sort of breakdown. He was going to send her home for the rest of the term and refer her to her local psychiatric team. The problem was…'

Troubled by Rahma welling up and wiping away the tear rolling down her cheek, I forced down my anxiety. Suki put her arm around her.

'Essie jumped over the landing banister from the top floor of the school building,' Suki sounded croaky and emotional, 'and Tasha-chan saw it happen.'

I threw my hand to my mouth. 'Oh, my God! Poor Essie! And poor Tasha!'

Suki and Rahma nodded. 'It was awful,' said Rahma, grabbing a tissue from the box on her bedside table and blowing her nose. 'We were all affected, of course, had counsellors in and everything. Other people saw Essie fall, you see. Thankfully, Suki and me weren't there. From what we heard, there was blood everywhere and Tasha was carried away by one of the male teachers. She was sedated and put in the san, taken home by her parents that very day. She came back the next term, a shadow of what she used to be.'

Shell-shocked and shivering, I was sitting on the edge of my bed, my thin pyjamas and absent slippers not helping. I pulled my dressing-gown tightly round my shoulders.

'Was – was there a suicide note?'

'Apparently, yes,' said Suki, kissing an emotional Rahma on the head before sliding off the bed, kicking off her slippers and climbing under her own duvet. 'Naturally, we weren't told what was in it and you can imagine the fuss, months of it. The police were brought in and there was an inquest. The verdict was suicide.

How they kept it out of the press is anyone's guess. We were getting these frantic calls from Tasha, telling us she was going to the inquest and the funeral. Unfortunately for her, only the teachers and Essie's parents and family were allowed to attend. Tasha's parents had her admitted to a children's psych ward. It was bloody depressing for everyone, I can tell you.'

'Especially for Tasha,' added Rahma.

'Horrendous,' I muttered sadly.

'Yeah. Essie got in deep.'

I won't let that happen to me!

'It was over a year ago,' said Suki matter-of-factly. 'Done; finished. It's unlikely Tasha will ever really get over it, although we've been trying to help her move on. It hasn't been easy and we're scared to bring it up. She refused to go to counselling and take the antidepressants they gave her, saying they gave her diarrhoea. To be honest, I wish she'd stayed on them, they were helping *us* if not her.'

Suki yawned and Rahma shook her head at her.

'I suppose it's natural Tasha considers me to be an intruder,' I said dejectedly. I'd got over my horror of sharing a dead girl's space weeks ago, especially on discovering that Essie's bed and mattress had been removed the term she died. 'She must think I'd replaced Essie and I suppose I have in a way, moving in here. She's thawing towards me a bit now, though why she won't accept me and Danny is beyond me.'

'It's obvious, really, Cherry,' said Rahma sleepily. 'She blames that Cody for grooming Essie and she thinks Danny will do the same to you. It's no wonder she disapproves of social media and online relationships and frankly, I agree. Each to their own, though,' she added hurriedly.

'Huh,' said Suki.

I was surprised and touched by this. 'Has Tasha said that?'

'Not specifically,' said Suki. 'She said the same to Essie and tried to find signs in her Pictapost and other social media accounts. Rahma and me were also close to Essie, of course, and her posts weren't suggestive and exhibitionist, unlike some people's.' That slutty schoolgirl pic came to mind and my skin went warm. 'Tasha tried to get into Essie's Pictapost to see what kind of messages had been sent between her and Cody. None of the passwords she attempted worked and in any case, his account was deleted in the end.'

Urging my panic to go away, I climbed into bed.

'So she never really found out what was upsetting Essie,' I said, 'what was going through her mind.'

'No,' said Rahma, 'and it's been haunting her ever since. The rest of us gave up on our conspiracy theories ages ago.' She rested her head against her pillow and suppressed a yawn. 'There you go, Cherry, that's the story from beginning to end. Don't let on to Tasha we told you, will you? She won't forgive us if she finds out. You didn't hear it from us,' she added, tapping her nose warningly.

'Tasha might tell Cherry one day,' said Suki.

'Perhaps she will,' said Rahma. 'That's up to Tasha, not us. It's very raw for her, Suki. She doesn't want people gossiping and everyone respects that.'

Suki sniffed again, plumped up her pillow and slammed her head against it. 'Yeah, whatever! Goodnight, my darlings. Sweet dreams and all that sort of thing.'

Rahma put her tongue out at her back and winked at me.

'Goodnight, Suki-the-pest. Goodnight, Cherry.'

My mind full of Tasha's awful anguish, sleep eluded me that night. To see Essie change from a bubbly, happy girl to a shadow of what she'd been, keeping everyone in the dark, and to take her own life, must have been heart-breaking and painful, especially for Tasha. How did you get over that easily and move on?

I'm not sure I'd have the strength.

Rahma and Suki hadn't mentioned whether Essie's Pictapost account was still visible; however, I resisted trying to find out in case I came across as nosey. I'd read somewhere it took years for a social media account of a dead person to be taken down: a girl at my old school had lost a cousin to leukaemia three years ago and the Facebook account remained active. People added comments on her birthday and at Christmas, sharing memories, telling her they loved and missed her, and I hoped people were doing the same for Essie.

At least Tasha had cheered up a fair bit thanks to the party; she was more cheerful, encouraging optimism for her mental health. On the Sunday evening, I wandered into the common-room in search of a book I'd left lying around somewhere and there she was, greeting me jovially.

'Nice weekend, Tasha?' I enquired breezily, determined to put our last clash over Danny behind me. She was lounging in a chair surfing her phone, having returned from a weekend break at home. Another girl was sitting at the table, typing on a laptop and wearing headphones.

'Yes, thanks. It was great seeing my mates again. They go to different schools and I miss them.' Tasha paused. 'I know you miss your mates at home, too. Do you keep in touch?'

Unable to see my book anywhere, I shrugged. I hadn't heard from Precious and Suze in ages and hadn't given them much thought, either; these days, I preferred my online world. Tulip was my home bestie these days and what she'd said to my news concerning Danny had been disappointing: 'Please take care, *cariad*.'

Irritation had surfaced again and I promptly changed the subject.

Ah, some kind soul had put my book away on the bookcase.

'No more than I used to. It is what it is. People tend to drift apart, I suppose.'

Tasha nodded and turned back to her phone. 'Yeah, it is what it is,' she agreed, adding, 'and it's probably your fault for spending most of your waking hours yapping to Danny, eh?'

I nearly dropped the book, trying to stay calm. 'What's that supposed to mean?'

'Nothing, really. How many followers has he got?'

'A few.' I was indignant now. 'Say it, Tasha. You think I'm wasting my life on Danny. I'm not, see. We're in a real relationship and we've fallen for one another.'

We're in love.

She showed me her phone screen, displaying Danny's Pictapost list.

'There are a hundred and eighty-three girls and young women on his list including you. What does that tell you?'

I blushed. 'It tells me he has girls on his list. Danny's an attractive bloke. What's your point, Tasha? He talks to lads, too.' *I must check that.* 'The main thing is he fancies *me*.'

'He probably tells other girls that.'

'Danny isn't...'

'Danny isn't what?'

'Nothing!' I said confusedly and left.

Danny isn't Cody.

It was at that point I pondered: was Tasha Ceridwen?

Eight
Adam

'Well done, Fisher!'

I waved my bat in appreciation at the applause and cheers from the spectators. Consistent sixes and fours had helped to score the century, and I was finally bowled out for one hundred and five. People patted me on the back as I strolled to the pavilion, removing my helmet and undoing my gloves.

Buzzing, Aziz gave me the thumbs up. 'We're going to win the House Cup and it's all thanks to you!'

He grabbed my waist in a bear hug and I laughed, caught up in his excitement.

I hadn't lost my talent for batting and over the last couple of weeks I'd helped Stanthorpe House win every fixture in an intense late summer Inter-House Cup competition, resulting in the folks in my class being a lot pallier. They no longer called me The Colonial and I was now plain 'Fisher'. I put away my helmet and faceguard, bat, gloves and pads in the changing-room equipment closet and went out to see the remainder of the match. We'd beaten Cranston House by five runs.

'Photos for Pictapost,' cried Petrov and we grouped together for a team snap. Later, the teacher managing the school account posted the photo and the score and Petrov, the proud scorer of thirty-eight runs, posted selfies and photos of some of his teammates on his own Pictapost profile, which, regardless of Crane's insistence, he hadn't closed down.

'He has no right to force me to delete it,' Petrov had grumbled in the dining-room later. 'The man doesn't own me, I have rights.' He added to me, 'Did Crane tell you to take down yours?'

I helped myself to potatoes and without looking at him stated, 'No, he grassed me up to the mods.'

Petrov had had the grace to shut up and look remorseful. Freddie Carlton-Greene changed the subject to rugby and my Pictapost drama was dropped.

The team photo done, I went back to the pavilion to get showered and changed. Petrov grabbed my arm and pulled me into a selfie with him, Carlton-Greene and Aziz.

'Odd that a Russian and an American have to show the Brits how to play cricket!' he remarked, showing us the picture.

Carlton-Greene groused and Aziz laughed, saying, 'Haven't you noticed that we're kind of light on Brits at The Priory, Petrov? We have to take what we can get, including you.'

Petrov stuck his tongue out at him. I approved how Aziz stood up to Petrov. It was easy to like him; he was a popular guy and always had a great collection of put-downs, especially where Petrov was concerned, and Petrov always took Aziz's opinions on his shortcomings better than anyone else's. I brooded over their relationship: did they have a closer bond than friendship?

Later at tea, Aziz said to me, 'Are you going to set up on Pictapost again, Fisher?'

'I haven't decided.'

'Don't let Crane put you off. I'll friend you.'

'What's that?' Carlton-Greene cut in. 'Are there any more horny girls on your Pictapost list, Fisher?' He gave Petrov a sly nudge. 'Send some my way.'

'My account got deleted,' I reminded him.

'So it did. Why?'

'Oh, keep up, CG,' said Aziz.

Petrov averted his gaze and continued to drink his tea.

Carlton-Greene pouted in disappointment. 'That's a bit harsh. Crane can't stop you setting up again. If you do, I'll add my name to your list.'

'You will?'

'Of course, especially if I can see pictures of gorgeous girls.'

Through a mouthful of ham sandwich, I said to Petrov, 'And you?'

'Me?'

Aziz chuckled. 'Petrov hacked into your phone and you'd trust him on social media?'

'Why not? You do, and he got you set up on that porn site.'

'HAHA!' Petrov smacked his hand on the table. 'He got you there, Aziz!'

'He did.' Aziz smiled. 'Go on, put us out of our misery, Fisher, will you set up a new account or not?'

'Dunno.'

'If you do, my handle is Azizee.' Aziz wrote it down on a paper napkin.

'I'm FCG100,' said Carlton-Greene.

'I'm…' began Petrov.

'I already know.'

'Really? Right, I guess I'll see you there,' he said, and for some reason, his wink turned my legs to jelly.

To set up a new Pictapost profile, I had to choose a different email address and at Scott's suggestion I used a VPN to hide my IP address to prevent the moderators tracing me that way. I also had to think up a new name. I jotted down a few ideas and decided on @alfish2008, using the first two letters of my initials (Lawrence was my middle name), part of my surname and 2008, the year I was born. Reluctant to be identified by previous contacts, other than Scott, Dean and my other pals, I decided not to use a profile picture of me and avoided any references to The Priory and the school account. I sent Scott and Dean quick messages.

'Dude!' Winking face and tongue out emoji from Scott. 'It's great to see you back online!'

'Nice to see you again,' chipped in Dean. 'How's school these days?'

I tapped my keypad eagerly, 'Missed you both! Yeah, school's all right, thanks. Things are better than they were. Petrov apologised for tagging Cherry's pic, Aziz told him to. Aziz is a great kid. He's also Petrov's best mate and takes no shit from him.'

'Why the boring avatar?' questioned Scott.

It was a picture of the Statue of Liberty I'd copied from Google Images to show I was American.

'It's best if I remain anonymous, at least for now. I daren't run the risk of being kicked off the site again.'

'There's no technology to id pics,' Dean pointed out. 'If they did, they'd take down a scam account straightaway, and they won't unless someone squeals on you, and forget the advice the anti-scammers give you, reverse image searching on Google isn't all that great, either.'

'I'm not taking that chance, Dean.'

All it took was for me to be recognised by somebody and for them to report me to the mods. I was taking a big risk allowing my schoolmates to see my new profile; it was difficult enough letting my guard down around them in real life.

Speaking to Scott and Dean on video cheered me up and I sent requests to some of my previous contacts, lying to them by telling them my old account had been hacked, apologising for the non-posts, unfriending if I heard nothing back. In two days, my list expanded. I put off contacting Cherry, worried she'd block me. Annoyingly, she hadn't changed her account to public and all I saw was her avatar, light flares filtering her selfie, enhancing her beautiful features, and my heart skipped more than a few beats. I often kissed that picture, kisses of affection and also a silent apology for what had happened.

A few weeks later, I kissed it again using a fake profile.

Petrov, Aziz and Carlton-Greene accepted my requests and they weren't impressed by my lack of posts, either.

'Isn't there *anything* you can upload?' demanded Carlton-Greene, obviously hoping to see a sexy pic. 'Where are all the girls?'

'Give me a chance, dude, it's a new account.'

'Shush,' said Aziz, his attention on an English TV show my mom liked called *Coronation Street,* a big favourite in our common-room. During the commercials, Aziz went to the kettle to make a round of tea and coffee and said, 'If you're that desperate to see pictures of girls in the nip, CG, you find some.'

'He does,' chipped in Petrov, blowing out vape smoke. 'He messages them, using his titled background to try and impress them. They call him a creepy catfish and block him. It's no more than he deserves.'

Everyone laughed at Carlton-Greene's discomfort. In fact, he was quite popular on Pictapost and had over two thousand people on his list, not all of them girls. He was honest, not pretending to be anyone more than a stocky and not particularly attractive young man.

'They do not!' he retorted indignantly. 'For your information, Daniil Petrov, I get on with all of them.'

'Especially the ugly ones, eh, Freddie?' chuckled Petrov, clearly enjoying Carlton-Greene's annoyance.

That earned him a splash of paint flicked from Carlton-Greene's paintbrush. A promising artist, he was painting from a postcard of a view in France for his mom's birthday in memory of their last vacation there.

Now it was Petrov's turn to be furious. 'Do that again and I'll ruin that precious painting of yours!' he threatened, irritably swiping the back of his hand across the spots of red paint that had landed on him, and realising his shirt and sweater were also affected, he whipped them off and threw them at Carlton-Greene, revealing his athletic chest and earning a few wolf whistles around the room. 'I'll let you put those in the washing-machine.'

Sticking his tongue out, Carlton-Greene pushed the shirt and sweater to one side. Petrov sat down at the table and took a selfie on his phone. On the TV, the commercials ended and the theme tune for *Coronation Street* hushed the room into silence, broken by Carlton-Greene remarking, 'You really are a poser, Dan Petrov!'

'SHUSH!' everyone hissed and Carlton-Greene snorted and shushed. I caught a glimpse of Aziz sipping his coffee and slyly glancing at the shirtless and apparently oblivious Petrov. I was surprised to find how much I also appreciated the Russian's physique and at that moment he became amusedly aware of my interest. I cleared my throat and hurriedly turned my attention to the TV.

The first opportunity I got to study Petrov's Pictapost profile was at bed, a favourite time for reading texts, Whatsapps from girlfriends and boyfriends and family and going onto Zoom, Facebook, Twitter and other social media platforms. Petrov's latest post got ninety-three Likes including from Aziz and Carlton-Greene, and from me. I took a snapshot of it to add to my collection, the fifth photo of his I'd copied to my gallery and I imagined Aziz having a collection of his own of Petrov's snaps, especially ones of him posing semi-naked, easy on the eye, a great crop of images. Carlton-Greene was right: Petrov had a massive ego and his photos appealed to the girls, judging by the comments I read.

It went without saying no one must ever find out my intention to get revenge on the guy I figured had messed up my chances of romance. Cherry had trusted me, now she decided I was a creepy catfishing perv and to be fair, I was becoming one. I was finding the shame of my actions difficult to bear and annoyingly, Petrov was beginning to trust and, surprise, surprise, tolerate me, and I was tolerating Petrov. These days I found it almost impossible to hate him for tagging that snap of Cherry, but I had to have justice, payback for what he'd done, ruining our relationship. The part of me that did hate him was winning by a nose, and that was why I had no qualms inventing Danny Roberts aka @dannyrob543, using Petrov's images.

I harvested pictures of Petrov's visit to Los Angeles, turning Daniil Petrov into Danny Roberts from California. The surname I'd chosen from Petrov's middle name, Robert. I was out to cause mischief, give Danny online exposure to girls and women, message them, lead them on, get the real Petrov notorious online and turn him into a scamming love rat. I had to wait it out, bide my time. Revenge was a dish best served cold. There was no rush. I needed to hook one girl and take it from there.

That girl turned out to be Cherry, not planned, it just happened. Now I was no longer Adam, I had an alter ego and I intended to send her a request in the hope she accepted, for me to see her posts. It worked and I was surprised at how swiftly she engaged. I was happy and dismayed: happy to see her and be in her life again, and more than slightly put out it was Petrov's image she was falling for, not mine.

Pushing away the disappointment and remorse from my mind, I posted a picture of Petrov waist deep in a river holding a fishing-rod.

'I said put that phone away, Fisher,' said the prefect on duty. 'Lights are going out.'

The next morning Aziz came running into my dorm hunting for Carlton-Greene, again the last one out of bed. The bell had already gone and he hadn't moved back his covers. The usual solution was to tip a glass of water over him and drag him out, a ritual he endured almost daily.

'What's wrong, man?' I said to Aziz, his demeanour fearful. 'You're spooked.'

He ignored me and went straight to Carlton-Greene's bed.

'CG! *Freddie!* Wake up, you lazy bugger!'

Carlton-Greene grumbled. 'Where's the fire, for Christ's sake?'

'Chocolate!' Aziz opened the drawer to Carlton-Greene's locker. 'Do you have any?'

Carlton-Greene was wide awake now. He shot out of bed and tried to prise the Mars Bar Aziz had found at the back of his drawer from his hand.

'Hey! I was saving that!' he protested.

'It's Petrov!' said Aziz, running back to the door. 'He's collapsed. He's having a hypo and he's out of chocolate!'

'Oh, shit!'

'Collapsed!' I gasped. *Why am I bothered?* 'Why? And what's the chocolate for?'

Carlton-Greene was now fishing for his dressing-gown. 'Petrov's diabetic,' he said. 'He gets these episodes and we have a chocolate drill for him to bring him out of it.'

The members of our dorm crowded next door. A drowsy and pale Petrov was lying on the carpet by his bed on his side, a pillow under his head, and everyone gathered round to witness Mr Jenson take his pulse.

'Have you got the chocolate, Aziz?' he barked. Aziz produced the bar, his hand trembling. Jenson tore off the wrapper and commanded, 'Sit him up.'

Instinctively, I darted forward and helped Aziz raise Petrov into a sitting position. Jenson forced a small piece of chocolate in Petrov's mouth, ignoring his groans of protest. 'Come on, lad,' Petrov chewed it slowly, 'that's it.' To the rest of the gathering he added, 'Can one of you call Matron, please?'

Carlton-Greene obliged. It took a few more pieces of chocolate before Petrov opened his eyes fully.

'What – what's happening?' he slurred. Aziz readily enlightened him.

'Lie down for a moment,' said Jenson. 'Good lad. Matron will be here shortly. You're not fit for classes today.'

Petrov settled his head on my lap. Now properly awake, he focused piercingly on me, his lips curled up in a smirk.

'You have really comfortable thighs, Fisher.'

Nine
Cherry

I told Danny if he dared treat me the way that Cody had treated Essie, I'd fly to Los Angeles, track him down and kill him.

'Where's this coming from, baby?' he wrote. He always called me 'baby' and 'my Queen'. I found the second preferable to the first; 'baby' was a bit too American for me. I had a nickname for him, calling him my Beautiful Brown-Eyed Baby Boy. If Suki, Rahma and Tasha found out, they'd take the mick.

'From a girl in school, warning me about a catfishing scumbag called Cody,' I told him. 'She said he was the reason her mate died.'

'That's awful. What happened?'

I gave him part of the story: that Essie had taken her own life over Cody.

'I'm very sorry,' said Danny. 'I won't hurt you, my queen, honestly.'

'That's right,' I said aloud. 'I won't bloody let you!'

Danny was on my mind 24/7 and I was truly, madly and deeply in love. Most of my days and nights were spent drooling over him and he helped me get through the long, dreary days at school. Was he legit? Ceridwen said he was a liar and a fake and despite my irritation that she remained a pest, her comments pricked at my conscience. What if she was right? Was that it: Ceridwen had been catfished in the past and was trying to warn me? I received no confirmation of that and anyway, I didn't need to be warned, I was determined not to be catfished and quite able to smell a creep and a perv a mile off. Greg and Jeremy were pervs and I'd had my fair share of uncomfortable encounters on Pictapost. The first sign of dodgy behaviour from Danny I'd drop him from a great height. I said the same to Tulip, confused by how vocal her warnings were.

'No need to worry,' Danny said. 'I'd never hurt you. Pay no mind to that stupid Ceridwen troll! Send me a snap. Please, baby? Let me sleep dreaming of you.'

Although it was against the rules to wear make-up on a weekday, I kept a lipstick in my pocket, cherry red, of course. It was near the end of break and I had a few moments to get to the toilets to take the photo. There was no one else around and to avoid being interrupted I nipped into a cubicle, applied the lippy and pouted at my camera phone. The result was a bit disappointing, but there was no chance to take another; the class bell had gone and I had to dash to Geography.

Everyone was already in their seats. I stumbled through the door of the classroom and Mr Ragnarsson frowned at me in disapproval, causing my tummy to flutter and my cheeks to puff out. Ragnarsson was in his late twenties, Norwegian, tall, athletic, strict, blond, engaged to a teacher from a neighbouring school and absolutely drop-dead gorgeous. Nearly every girl at Helton worshipped the ground he walked on, me included.

'Thank you for joining us, Cheralyn!' he said sarcastically. The class giggled. I yanked my cardigan free from the door handle and legged it to my desk, my cheeks blazing.

'I'm only a minute late,' I muttered inaudibly.

'Come here,' he ordered.

Now what?

Catching Suki almost bursting into laughter, I dumped my bag on the floor, steadied my composure, and obeyed Ragnarsson's command, my knees knocking.

'Yes, Mr Ragnarsson?' I said innocently.

'Is that lipstick you're wearing?' *Oh, shit, I'd forgotten to wipe the damn stuff off!* Mr Ragnarsson took a tissue out of the box on his desk and handed it to me. 'Get rid of it and stay behind after class, please.'

I scuttled back to my desk and heard Rahma murmur, 'Have a wet wipe. The lipstick's smudged.' She secreted a wipe onto my lap.

'Thanks,' I muttered. People were grinning at me and Ragnarsson banged on his desk.

'Pay attention, you lot. Open your textbooks to chapter seven.'

Later, Ragnarsson's lecture over, Suki, Rahma and Tasha waited for me outside the classroom and Rahma said, 'Why the lippy?'

Embarrassed, I tried to think up an excuse, but Tasha got there first.

'Why do you think?' she said coldly. 'It's for Danny. She's been taking photos for him, haven't you, Cherry?'

I was immediately on the defensive. 'And? I'm always sending him pictures.'

'It's dangerous and if you get caught...'

'Oh, get off your high horse, Tasha!' Suki jumped in impatiently. 'Since when did school rules ever bother you? You're always sneaking off into town to buy fags.'

Tasha went pale. Rahma had told me Essie's death had turned Tasha into a secret smoker. It upset her and Suki and it was a miracle she hadn't been caught. Being under age, how was she getting her hands on them? She had packets of fags hidden in her bag, at the back of her knicker drawer and under her mattress.

Tasha had recovered her senses and snapped, 'It's none of your business, Suki Ito, and you have no call to judge me, the amount of drink you put away! You're practically an alcoholic!'

Suki narrowed her lovely brown eyes, hitched her bag onto her shoulder, folded her arms and took a step towards Tasha. 'The difference between you and me is, Tash,' she said slowly, 'at least I wait for the weekend. You must smoke at least twenty a day; and no amount of showering, changing your uniform and drowning your arse in body spray and perfume can get rid of the smell of fag ash! It lingers and I bet you any money the teachers have noticed.'

She marched off. 'Bye,' called Rahma. Suki was a champion sulker and Rahma's advice was to leave her to it. Tasha sniffed and stalked away in the opposite direction. I shook my head at Rahma helplessly. It was going to be frosty in the common-room and in our dorm later.

There was no point trying to convince Tasha, she refused to listen and avoided me and Suki all day.

Was Tasha Ceridwen? 'You're playing with fire!' being an example of the persistent messages she kept leaving, and did I want to run the risk of confronting her and getting into another argument? Things were already strained between us. I decided to wait a bit longer, see what else had been posted and commented.

The Ceridwen profile remained blank: no avatar, no posts, no friends, and following one person: me. It was all very strange. I resented Tasha's attitude towards Danny and it made me more determined not to give him up. During Geography, he'd sent me another picture of him, shirtless: 'All for you, baby.' Oh, those beautiful brown peepers! I crossed my legs, the familiar tingling of longing for him coursing through my veins.

'Sweet Jesus,' I muttered. 'You're gorgeous!'

I noticed a comment from Ceridwen on Danny's new post of him posing fishing in a river: 'Liar. You don't exist.' Danny obviously hadn't seen it, he would have deleted it. Irritated, I removed the comment as the History teacher came in and later kissed the love emoji Danny sent.

It was a problem living in a different part of the world to Danny, daylight for him during the night for me and vice versa, and him messaging me while it was the early hours across the ocean gave me a warm glow inside. Los Angeles was eight hours behind the UK and understandably he couldn't stay online for long. Where was the harm in an early hour rendezvous if I happened to wake up?

A week later a badly-sprained ankle in hockey practice did prevent me from sleeping, thanks to Clarissa Cleverley's hockey stick, smacking me on the shin and sending me flying to the turf, landing awkwardly, prompting Mrs Li, the sports teacher, to come running over, blowing her whistle, and ordering a dischuffed Clarissa off the field.

'Are you badly hurt, Cheralyn?' I was clutching my ankle and clenching my teeth at Mrs Li gently taking off my boot and inspecting the damage. It was already starting to bruise and swell up. 'Hmm, it's probably a sprain, not a fracture.' She took her mobile phone out of her pocket.

'Karen is on her way over. Stay where you are, Cheralyn. You're safer there for now.'

The grass was damp and I was glad Karen, one of the assistant matrons, arrived five minutes later. She nodded at my swelling and bruised ankle and agreed that an x-ray was a good idea. 'I'll bring my car round. Do you think you can stand, Cheralyn?'

'Come on, Tash, let's give her a hand,' Suki instructed, and they took an arm each to get me up.

At the hospital, the doctor confirmed the sprain. 'No sport for you for at least six weeks, Cherry,' she instructed.

She put a compress bandage around my foot and gave Karen a packet of prescription painkillers. I was to rest for a few days and gradually weight bear gently.

'Keep your foot elevated and apply an ice pack to it,' she added.

'You'd better spend tonight in the san,' said Karen, helping me into the main school building where the san was. 'We'll go straight there and get you comfortable. Nadia is on call this evening. If you're in any pain in the night she can give you more tablets.' She saw my lack of excitement and added, 'You won't be bored. There's a telly and I'll fetch whatever prep you have to do, and you'll have your phone.'

She also brought my PJs, toiletries, toothbrush, magazine, book and phone charger, and also, such a lovely surprise, chocolate and a bottle of Pepsi from Rahma, Suki and Tasha, really sweet of them. The best news of all was my year tutor had let me off prep.

The san was a bright room comprising of six beds, the odd painting adorning the white walls, one occupant (me) and a forty inch HD telly to keep me company.

'I'm off to ring the kitchen to have some supper sent up for you,' said Karen, putting a pillow on the footrest. 'Sit in the comfy chair and keep your foot raised on there. I'll be back shortly. How's the pain?'

'Bearable.'

'Good.' She placed the ice pack on my ankle. *OO, cold!* 'You're not allowed any more pain relief for two hours and the ice will help bring the swelling down.'

I waited for her to leave the room, got into my pyjamas and logged into Pictapost: a couple of messages from Rahma, Suki and Tasha and men begging me to send them naked photos (blocked), nothing from Danny. I'd already taken some pictures of my foot, now already black and blue, and sent them to him, adding a sad emoji. I was gutted not to hear back from him and then reminded myself it was the middle of the night over there. I tried to concentrate on the telly, glancing at my phone at intervals. By nine-thirty and bed, I was on edge. Why hadn't he been in touch? Nadia, the other assistant matron, took over from Karen at nine o'clock and ordered me into bed. Once alone, I tried to take my mind off

Danny by tormenting a man who'd messaged me: 'Hi. What's your name? Where are you from?' leading him on and finally blocking him. At last, yawning, I dropped off to sleep. At ten-past one according to the clock on the wall, my ankle woke me up and I rang the bell for Nadia.

There was a message waiting for me on Pictapost. 'Baby,' it said.

I waited impatiently for Nadia to finish administering my painkillers and leave the room, grabbed my phone and tapped, 'Hi there, my Beautiful Brown-Eyed Baby Boy!'

Ten
Adam

'I won't hurt you, my queen.'

That was probably the tenth reassuring note I'd sent to Cherry, I'd lost count. She was getting edgy, needy, doubting. It was kind of frustrating and not helped by the comments left by that weird Ceridwen. I was tired of this troll calling me a fake and a catfish, whether it was true or not. No sooner was the account taken down than another turned up posting more accusing comments. I had to prevent Cherry from believing I was another Cody. If I overplayed my hand and hassled her too soon, she'd walk away and probably block me. I had to be careful.

I knew I *was* hurting Cherry really. She didn't know me from Adam, no pun intended. Ceridwen was right: Cherry had fallen for a fake called dannyrob543, AKA Adam Fisher, calling me her Beautiful Brown-Eyed Baby Boy; in reality my eyes were green. I was a fraud and hated myself for it. The desire to get back at Petrov was winning against the remorse I harboured for cheating Cherry; nevertheless, the best way for me to contact her again was by being a different person, using Petrov's images, a way back into her life. We were messaging one another regularly and sharing snaps, nothing racy; it was early days to harass her into sending me more explicit stuff and scare her off, whereas I happily contributed topless, yet tasteful, photos of 'Danny'. I had to acknowledge the fact I was no longer @adamfishofficial and my happiness was confused by a warped sense of anger that she'd got over the real me pretty fast and had fallen for a phony. She'd moved on and it rankled. Meanwhile, our new online relationship went on and she was getting more and more into Danny, and there was a part of me intent on punishing her for forgetting Adam Fisher.

Considering Cherry believed I lived in Los Angeles, eight hours behind the UK, I saved messaging till late in the evening, that way she'd think it was afternoon in the US. My phone buzzed at around one in the morning and woke me out of one of my frequent, regret-filled dozes that often plagued me. Things kept going round and round in my head: how I was going to use Petrov's photos to get him into hot water…

…and what will I do if I'm ever caught!

Carefully, I opened my bedside drawer and took out my phone, ducking under the duvet to keep the screen light from disturbing the others. Dean had sent a photo of himself at the beach clutching his surfboard and I wished I was there, thinking of all the happy hours me and my pals had spent swimming and surfing. Dean was a ripped, handsome dude and wasted on members of the same gender.

I turned my attention to the snaps Cherry had sent of her foot earlier and was alarmed at how swollen and bruised it was. I hadn't messaged on purpose, deciding for now Danny's motto should be 'Treat 'em mean, keep 'em keen.' She'd sent three messages, accompanied by four crying emojis, telling me how painful her ankle was.

'Sorry I'm late getting back to you, baby,' I wrote guiltily. 'It's very busy at work at the moment in the bank. I'm sorry you hurt your ankle. Kiss for you, baby.'

I was surprised by the immediate: 'It's fine, sexy. I'll forgive you anything.'

I sniggered, loving her calling me 'sexy'. 'Why are you awake now? It must be late over there.'

'Yeah, it's gone one o'clock in the morning and I can't sleep. The pain in my foot is pretty bad.'

'Have you taken any drugs for it?'

'Naproxen. It's not working yet. I think I need a strong drink to deaden the agony.'

'Send me a snap, baby,' I pleaded, 'in all your beautiful glory. Please.'

'What, now?'

'Yeah.'

'Nadia might come in if I put the lamp on. She's the assistant matron on call tonight.'

'You can use the flash on your phone.'

'Nah, you won't be able to see me properly.'

'Go on, baby.'

Shortly, a photo came through of her posing at the camera, still pale and beautiful under the haze of the lamp. I tittered at the hint of a bare shoulder and her pout. I had her eating out of the palm of my hand and I loved that power, all the while despising my deceit.

'You're lovely,' I wrote.

'No, I'm not.'

'You are. You're the most beautiful girl I've ever seen.'

'It's not a great picture. I took half a dozen and that's the best one.'

We stayed online for a bit longer, discussing my 'work' at the 'bank', her school, our hobbies, our interests and swapping silly love notes. Eventually, feeling jaded and tired, something crazy prompted me to type, totally unexpectedly and randomly, 'I have to tell you about Christina, baby.'

Speedily, she was back at me: 'Is she your girlfriend?'

'No, my queen, Christina's my daughter.'

Christina was actually Petrov's small sister Katia, invented on a risky whim. Petrov had posted plenty of pictures of her, a cute kid of eleven, her long blonde hair tied in plaits. I was expecting a barrage of questioning that came very rapidly and imagined the fury behind her words.

'Your *daughter*?'

I sent Petrov's sister's photo and Cherry went silent.

'Her mom Caroline was a one-night stand.' The lies were getting easier and I detested every single one I told. 'I hardly see my daughter. She lives with my mom in Texas now and I visit twice a month.'

'Where's her mother?'

'She died in a car crash.'

'Oh, Jesus!'

'Yes.' I sighed for effect. 'I gave her a lift to the shopping mall…'

'Oh, no! How awful!'

'It all happened really fast and Caroline died in my arms.'

'Oh, shit, Danny! I'm sorry!'

'Thank you. It was two years ago. I'm kind of over it.'

'Oh. She's very pretty.'

'Thanks.' *Get her off the subject.* 'Are the painkillers working now, my queen?'

'Yes, the pain's going. Listen, it's getting on for two o'clock here.'

'In that case, go to sleep now, baby. Will you do that for me?'

'Yes. I suppose if I stay up any longer I won't be fit to be seen tomorrow – I mean today.'

'I have to go. I have to get dinner and I'm going out tonight.'

'Where?'

'To a bar.'

'Oh?'

'Yeah, I'm meeting some guys from the bank.'

'And girls?'

'No.' Unamused face emoji. 'Why all the questions, baby? It's all what I'm doing and what I'm up to, who I'm seeing and who I'm messaging.'

I came across irritated and I was. Her interrogation was getting to me, even if she had good reason to be suspicious of me: hadn't I landed a fake daughter on her out of the blue?

'What a hypocrite you are!' she snapped back. 'You question me!'

'I question *you?*'

'Do I message this guy, do I message that guy…'

The blood pounded in my ears.

And now you tell me you have a bloody daughter! Full of surprises, aren't you?'

I was stunned by her aggression.

'I'm sorry, baby,' was all I managed.

So much for: 'I'll forgive you anything.'

'I'm tired,' she said. 'I'm going to sleep now.'

'Sleep well, baby. Speak tomorrow?'

She went offline.

Scowling, I switched off the phone, put it under my pillow and tried to go to sleep.

***

I was the last to get out of bed the next morning. Carlton-Greene was up and partially dressed before I uttered a grunt of despair and pushed back my duvet. I'd slept heavily, haunted by self-reproach, despising my deception of a girl who'd done me no harm and I was in serious doubt whether it was worth it. Maybe not; and the thaw in relations between Petrov and me meant it was more difficult to justify carrying on my plan for vengeance, especially now life at The Priory was easier. Perhaps I should forget it, take down the fake account, be Adam again and contact Cherry, saying I was sorry and was she willing for us to get together. The problem was, she was into Danny now – under the guise of Petrov – and she'd fallen for him from a great height.

What a snake I am.

It took me ages to find a clean pair of socks and I was one of the last stragglers into the dining-hall for breakfast. Cherry had been online and posted a snap on her page showing off her bandaged foot. She'd ignored my 'Hi baby' and love emoji and that spoilt my mood, resulting in very little sleep that night. The next day, I was pulled up in virtually every lesson for staring out of the window. It was a big risk getting my phone out to see whether Cherry had messaged me.

'What's the matter, Fisher?' Aziz nudged me during prep. 'You've been weird and snappy all day.'

'Nothing; I slept badly, is all.' I'd been caught by Crane nodding off in German class.

'What did Crane say?'

'Not much. I have to be in bed an hour early tonight and have extra German prep on Saturday morning.'

'Bad luck,' said Aziz sympathetically.

I tried to settle down to work, congratulating my willpower on having resisted the urge to log into Pictapost until supper. There being no word from Cherry, I was forced to reach the conclusion she was ghosting me. Oh, so what? My list was full of girls to choose from.

Another message from that Ceridwen: 'She's onto you. She's sussed you out for what you really are.' I swore back and blocked her.

Dog-tired, I was glad to crawl into bed at eight that evening and slept through the usual noise from the others coming into the dorm, dreaming I heard chuckling and felt prodding in my back.

'Oh, leave him alone and get into bed, CG!' said someone impatiently and I slept dreamlessly for the rest of the night.

Eleven
Cherry

We'd both had a gutful of Ceridwen!

She was everywhere, always leaving comments on Danny's posts, calling him a catfish. I was also sick to death of Danny's daughter, this Christina, who kept preying on my mind. Granted she was a pretty little girl and resembled him, but she was surely not his daughter, no way if she was eleven! Danny must be older than he said he was, twenty-nine not nineteen. I was ecstatic, an older man interested in me and if that was the case, it also meant he'd lied to me.

'Christina's happy I've met you,' he told me.

I said nothing. Ceridwen had commented on his latest post, one of him where he was hugging the kid: 'She's not your daughter and her name's not Christina.'

We both immediately blocked her, although I secretly agreed: no way was Danny old enough to be the girl's dad. Whoever the troll was had given up the @ceridwen handle in its various forms and now used random Pictapost names, signing their comments 'Ceridwen'.

'This person is a serious pain in the ass,' Danny wrote. 'Reporting and blocking them is no use.'

'I've a good mind to deactivate my account,' I said.

'What? No!'

'Have you got any better ideas?'

'Please, baby, don't leave me!'

'Why not switch to Facebook, or Twitter?' I replied impatiently.

'I'm not really into them.'

I inhaled deeply. 'Erm, I'll give you my phone number.' It was a massive risk and I was unsure if I was prepared for such a commitment.

'You'd do that for me?' he said.

Good question.

'Probably, later on,' I typed rapidly.

'Fair enough, baby.'

Suddenly, a notification came up that @dannyrob543 was opening a video chat, right in the middle of dinner break in the school dining-room. In danger of being caught by a teacher, I bottled it, closing my phone immediately. Tasha was shaking her head at me from across the dining-table. Later, in the common-room, Danny questioned why I'd ignored his call.

'I – I'm not ready for that, not yet. We've not known one another that long, have we?'

'Whatever you say, my queen.'

'Come on, Cherry-chan,' Suki said. The telly was switched off and everyone went to the door. The assistant teacher on duty had arrived to chivvy us to our rooms. 'Put Danny away now, your beauty sleep awaits.'

I obliged reluctantly. Rahma had texted to say she was on her way back from late football practice at the indoor pitch. The playing fields were buried in white; it had been snowing all day and there were steady snowflakes reflected in the orange glow of the lamps lighting the grounds. Tasha hadn't returned, either; she'd gone to the library to borrow a book for her science project and she hadn't come back.

I trailed behind Suki to our room, shivering from the effects of the cold. I'd been to the town to buy some toiletries, wrapped up against the bitter wind in my coat, scarf, gloves and woolly jumper. Nearly everyone on the street had been hanging onto railings, walls and lampposts to prevent slipping on the icy pavements. Hardly able to feel my hands, I was glad to warm them on the radiator in the hall, welcoming the hot tomato soup and bread served at supper.

'I'm not entirely certain Tasha went to the library,' Suki had said out of earshot of the others in the common-room. Supper had been an hour ago and Tasha remained absent. I'd heard nothing from Ceridwen all day, either. I continued to speculate if Tasha was Ceridwen and I was becoming more and more nervous at the idea of confronting her, to the point where I'd decided against it. 'I reckon she nipped into town to get fags. She's got none left. She was scrambling round her knicker drawer where she hides them, desperate to find some. She'll be in the shit if she's caught out of bounds.'

'She's mad if she's gone out in that tonight!'

'Let's hope she's back and already in bed.'

She wasn't. Rahma was alone in our room, her nose in a book.

'Good, thanks. Isn't she here?' was Rahma's reaction to Suki's questions: 'How was footie practice?' and 'Have you seen Tasha?'

'No. She's gone to the library, hasn't she?'

We looked at one another in silence. Suki rang Tasha's phone; it went straight to voicemail.

'Er...' began Rahma.

'I bet she's gone into town to get fags,' said Suki.

'She ought to have been back by now, though,' I said apprehensively. 'Do you think she's been caught breaking bounds?'

'It's possible she hasn't come back at all,' said Suki.

Rahma closed her book, threw back her duvet and climbed out of bed. Tasha's clothes and weekend case were in the wardrobe. 'I suppose we'd better go out and search for the pest.' She proceeded to pull on jeggings and a hoodie over her pyjamas, freaking at the tap on the door. The scarfed head belonging to Fatima Navid, the prefect on duty, popped her head in.

'Not in bed? Where's Tasha?'

'In the san,' I said quickly.

'Really? Why?'

'Dicky tummy,' chipped in Suki. 'She's been throwing up all day.'

'Urgh, the poor thing!'

'Yes,' said Rahma. At the door opening, she'd jumped back into bed in a panic in case whoever came in saw the bottom of her PJs under her jeggings. 'I think there's a bug going round. I'm a bit queasy, to be honest.'

'Really?' Fatima wrinkled her nose. 'All right, I'll be along in ten minutes to see if your lights are out; I won't come in again.' She was obviously scared she was going to catch this fictitious germ.

'Smart thinking, Cherry,' approved Rahma. 'I hope she doesn't bump into one of the matrons and asks how Tasha is.'

'Soz. It was all I could think of to say on the spur of the moment,' I defended.

'No harm done.'

'Wait,' said Suki, putting on her coat. 'What if Fatima tells Ragnarsson? He's on house duty tonight. Carter's at a conference and if he goes to see Tasha in the san...'

'Yeah, Suki, you're right!'

'We have to pray that he doesn't,' said Rahma, grabbing her boots. 'There's not much we can do now. Got your coats?'

We nodded. It was a good job we'd chosen to wear our home coats: I wore a navy winter raincoat, Rahma a black Burberry and Suki her brown cashmere, hoping the dark colours and our hoods kept us incognito on CCTV.

'We'd better switch off the light and wait a bit. If Ragnarsson does the sweep there'll be trouble,' Rahma went on. 'At least being a man he won't walk in without checking we're decent. Sharma charges in uninvited, doesn't she, Suki?'

'Oh, God, yeah, that time she caught me in my bra and pants!' Suki laughed.

'HAHA! What happened?' I said, kicking off my slippers and pulling on my boots.

'It was at the beginning of term. Sharma was standing in for Carter one weekend. Rahma and Tasha were away and I was alone in the room. Sharma barges in and tells me to hurry up and get into bed. I very nearly said to her, why, did she fancy joining me?'

We burst out laughing and shushed immediately at the sound of Ragnarsson speaking to Fatima in the corridor. Expecting a knock on our door, Suki signalled to our beds and we jumped under our duvets.

The voices faded away and relief washed over us.

'Give it five minutes,' whispered Rahma. 'Wait for the coast to be clear.'

So we waited.

'Are we heading into town?' I said at last.

'Best check the library first,' said Suki. The library was unstaffed from five o'clock and closed at ten. 'That's where Tasha said she was going.'

'Everyone except the staff and Sixth Form gets kicked out at five,' Rahma pointed out, 'unless she's risked it and is hiding in one of the computer rooms.'

We hadn't discussed what to do if we bumped into a member of staff coming out of the library, in its own small building in the grounds a few hundred yards down the drive from Rowan House; we were more concerned at how we were going to get to the ground floor and out of the building unseen. Most of the population of Rowan were in their rooms and it'd be our bad luck to get caught sneaking around by a prefect patrolling the building. Not only did Miss Carter live in Rowan, a handful of other staff did, too.

Suki carefully opened the door and peeped out, the light from her phone enough to guide our way through the darkness on the landing. We kept close together in our coats, scarves and gloves and away from the wall to avoid tripping over furniture.

At the stairwell we paused and listened.

'Anyone down there?' I mouthed.

'We'll soon find out, I suppose,' muttered Rahma. 'Let's go, and for goodness' sake don't make any noise.'

We crept down the stairs slowly, wincing at every stair creak, thanking our lucky stars for not bumping into anyone official on the way down and in the hall. On reaching the bottom step, however, we received a nasty surprise: the house mother's office door was open and the light was on.

Unsettled by the sight of Ragnarsson sitting on the sofa, surrounded by exercise books, pen in hand, taking sips from a bottle of beer and paying occasional attention to the telly, turned down low, we clutched one another, rooted to the spot, hardly daring to breathe. He had his own room in the main school building and must have been sleeping over in Rowan in Carter's absence. It was the end if he saw us in our coats. He picked up his buzzing phone from the coffee table and we seized the opportunity to leg it to the front exit. Suki slowly opened the squeaking door, causing us to cringe and hug one another. Mercifully, Ragnarsson was preoccupied on the phone and we escaped undetected.

'Phew,' muttered Suki.

'That was a close one,' agreed Rahma, carefully and quietly clicking the door behind her.

'Shouldn't we see if Tasha is in the Head's office?' I said, clinging to the hope Tasha was safely being roasted for breaking bounds and not lying in a ditch somewhere.

'It's not very likely, Panesar went to the conference with Carter,' said Suki.

We went straight to the library. Fortunately, the path had been gritted and we were able to walk without slipping and sliding. The last person out of the library building was supposed to switch off the computers and the lights and set the key code on the main door.

'She won't be on the second floor,' said Suki, staring up at the lights there. 'That's where the staff collection is and the code to get in is a state secret.'

We took it in turns to peek through the windows on the ground floor, preparing to duck down if anyone turned round and happened to glance in our direction. We saw five Sixth Formers browsing the shelves and reading. Tasha couldn't have remained inconspicuous for long in that company.

'Nah, she's not in there,' said Rahma. 'We'd better go and search around town.'

Using our phone lights again to guide our way, we took the preferred bound-breaking route – the worst-kept secret in the school – through the wooden fence at the back of the lower playing-field, a blind spot from the CCTV cameras and ground lights, camouflaged by bushes and small trees. Over the years the fence had been patched up in various places, badgers and foxes having been blamed for digging the earth underneath to scramble through, damaging the panels, and luckily, there were no recent repairs. We squeezed our way through a fairly large gap, where Suki snagged her leggings and Rahma lost her bobble hat in the little, partially-thawed stream trickling alongside. Fishing it out, she twisted it to rinse the water out and sulked over her hat and gloves getting wet.

'Clumsy,' Suki remarked, giggling.

Rahma snarled at her and stuffed the hat into a protesting Suki's pocket.

'I hope we find her soon,' I said, hurrying along past the train station into town. It was bitterly cold and snowing again and the breeze was blowing flakes in our faces. Our coats and scarves were turning white. 'It's that cold I think my nose will drop off and my gloves aren't making much difference to my poor hands! I'll kill Tasha if we freeze to death!'

'Uh?' Suki frowned at my impossible comment and I explained the joke. 'Oh, that's funny. What'll we do if we *can't* find her? Tell the police she's missing?'

'It hasn't come to that,' said Rahma, rolling her eyes at her.

'We have to cover all eventualities.'

'It won't do any good fretting about things that probably won't happen.'

'What if she's been kidnapped? It's dark and cold and there aren't that many people out tonight. There's a reason they won't let us out this late, Rahma, and most of us come from rich backgrounds. Imagine the ransom demands.'

'Oh, Jesus, Suki, quit catastrophising!' cried Rahma impatiently at Suki's overactive imagination and Suki stuck her tongue out at her.

In the high street, we searched the corner shops and the Tesco, still open, without success. Tasha remained elusive.

Suki said, 'What if she meant she was going to the public library, not the school library?'

'It closes at nine,' Rahma pointed out.

'What if she got locked inside somehow?' I said.

'If she had any sense she'd ring us for help,' said Suki. 'We can call the police and get her out; the problem is, sense never was Tasha's strong point. Let's try the park.'

The park was closed. Stumped, we stood in the middle of the pavement to ponder on the mystery of the missing Tasha.

'Where to next?' said Rahma.

My phone vibrated in my pocket. At first, thinking it was a notification from Danny on Pictapost, I ignored it; now was not the occasion for gushy messaging, then I realised it was actually a phone call.

'Tasha?'

'Cherry, thank Christ!'

'Tasha, where are you? We're out in the town looking for you.'

I put the phone on loudspeaker and Suki and Rahma moved closer.

'Tasha! Tasha-chan, you stupid cow, tell us where you are!' cried Suki.

'Hush, Suki!' said Rahma.

'Tasha?' I said.

'Oh, Cherry!' Tasha was starting to cry. 'There was no signal and…'

'No probs, you've got through to me now. Where are you? We'll come and get you.'

'Please hurry,' sobbed Tasha. 'I think I've killed him!'

Twelve
Adam

Helton was in the middle of nowhere. First, I had to get a train from Sudbury, the nearest station to The Priory, to London Liverpool Street, catch a tube to Euston, Euston to Kendal, and lastly a train from Kendal to Helton, departing once a day at three-thirty in the afternoon, and the entire journey took around five hours altogether. The school authorities assumed I was on my way home for the weekend when actually I planned to visit Cherry in Helton, the one person I yearned to see, needing the sort of comfort to be found in the arms of a beautiful girl.

And that girl had to be Cherry.

I'd overheard a lad at school telling his pals how he'd dated a girl last weekend at home and they'd gone all the way. His story made me lonelier for Cherry more than ever and I needed to go to Helton to hook up and begin a real relationship. I prayed she'd listen to my explanation and the apology I'd rehearsed, find it in her soul to forgive me for lying and pretending to her. Intending to surprise her, I imagined her shock and was curious to find out what she would do if Adam, not Danny, turned up, and if it worked out, I fully intended to abandon Danny and think of another way to get back at Petrov.

On a cold, snowy, dark evening at nearly four-fifteen, the train pulled into Helton Station. It had been a stressful journey and a sudden weird, niggling-type headache on board the tube at Euston had very nearly prompted me to turn back. I put it down to tension, swallowed two painkillers and, boosted by messages of love from Cherry to which I readily engaged, 'I love you, my queen!' I continued my onward journey. Stupidly, I hadn't figured out where I'd be staying or knew if I had to give proof of age to a hotel. Apparently, you had to be eighteen to stay unaccompanied in a lot of places in the UK. There were no YMCAs near Helton, either. It was a very small town.

Unsure of where to go, I stood at the entrance to the station and surveyed the traffic, people running for buses and the street lights shining on puddles of melted snow in the road. I shivered, cursing myself for not putting on a scarf and thick jumper and not studying the weather forecast properly before travelling. Knowing the weather was colder in the north, wearing merely a shirt, leather jacket and jeans had been an unwise move.

The headache had robbed me of my appetite and I'd not eaten on the train, only managing a coffee. Figuring it was sensible to eat, I decided to find a café, where maybe I'd find out if there were any digs nearby. I planned to turn in early; the nagging headache hadn't gone away and I longed for sleep. At a kiosk in the coach station, I bought a bottle of Pepsi and dragged my trolley case behind me, crossed the road and followed the signs downhill towards the town centre.

I passed a pub called The Jolly Miller that had rooms vacant. Not an option, I was underage. Across the road was a brown sign showing a picture of a bed: a hotel, half a mile further into town.

What to do, where to go?

And then she walked straight into me.

The girl's grey duffle coat was buttoned to the neck and the hood protected her from the falling snow. Around her neck she had a thick black scarf and her hands were hidden under a black fur muff. She was quite pretty: the cold had turned her cheeks and the tip of her nose pink and there were blonde highlights in her reddish-brown hair. What marred the delightful image was the distinct smell of cigarette smoke. She took out a hand to pull her hood firmly further over her head and snapped in her proper English accent, 'Watch where you're going!'

'Uh, what?' I retorted. 'You walked into *me!*'

She sniffed and brushed past me. I noticed a packet of cigarettes at my feet and called to her. 'Excuse me. Are these yours?'

She turned, marched towards me and snatched the packet from my hand.

'You're kinda rude!' I snapped.

'And Americans are a blight on the planet,' she said haughtily.

'Yeah? Whatever.' *Wait, if she's local...* 'Hey, do you live round here?'

She stopped again. 'Not far. What's it to you?'

'I'm looking for a place to stay.'

'In Helton?'

'Yeah.'

'Are you here alone?'

I nodded.

'You must be what, sixteen, seventeen?'

'I'm sixteen next month.'

'Whatever, what's a Yank doing in a small Lake District town?'

I winced. Another ignorant limey calling me a Yank!

'I'm – visiting a friend. She lives here. We – we're kind of pen-pals.'

'Have you come all the way from America to see her?'

I turned my head away and muttered, 'You Brits and your bloody questions.'

'I beg your pardon?'

'I said no, I live in the UK. I've come for the weekend.'

'What's the girl's name? Helton's a small place; it's possible I know her and she could go to my school. There are two other schools, but they're nearly two miles out of town. I'm at Helton Manor, in that direction.' She nodded towards the train station.

I dithered. What if she told Cherry and ruined the surprise?

'Helton Manor?'

'Yes.' She was staring at me intently, her head cocked to one side. 'I think you may have heard of it.'

'I – er...'

'She *is* a pupil there, isn't she? I bet it's Cherry Hill in my class. She messages an American on Pictapost. It's you, isn't it? I have to say the photos don't do you justice in the flesh. Your hair's lighter and she said you were older.' I cleared my throat and went red. 'Is she expecting you?'

Her triumphant, almost sinister manner was getting to me.

'I – was intending to surprise her,' I explained warily. 'I'm staying overnight and was hoping to meet her.'

The girl sniffed. 'Fair enough, I won't tell her. It's none of my business, anyway. It'll either be a terrible shock or a lovely surprise for her, you'll find out.'

That was one thing we did agree on.

'You've booked accommodation?' she added.

'No, I'm afraid not. I was hoping to just turn up to a place. The hotel will be expensive for me, I guess, and the pub will turn me away.'

'You haven't planned your visit properly, have you?'

Embarrassed, I said nothing.

'There's a guest house not far from here and they do get a few visitors in the winter,' she went on. 'They ought to have a room and they won't turn you away if you have the money to pay the bill.'

'Thank you. Where is it, please?'

'I'll take you there.'

Not having had any better offers, I trailed behind her like a trusting puppy, lugging my case behind me. We crossed the road to a side street and she walked a little ahead of me in silence, which suited us both. She annoyed me and neither of us was interested in the other's name. I was keen to get to wherever this accommodation was, dump my case, and find someplace to eat. Approaching a more residential area put doubts in my mind that this mysterious guest house actually existed. Surely it was in the opposite direction, in the town centre?

'Are we going the right way?' I enquired, breaking the silence. 'Isn't this place in the town?'

'No, it's near the lake, down the end of this road on the left.'

I took my phone out of my pocket and went onto Google. 'What's it called?'

'The Boathouse. It's close to the shore on Coniston Water and they rent out rowboats in high season.'

No results.

'I'm not sure if it has a website,' she said, observing me self-consciously surf my phone to find the place.

It was a boathouse, all right, clearly not a guest house, and an empty one at that. There were no cars parked outside and, apart from a grey-haired couple further along the shoreline, walking their dog in the other direction, the place was deserted. I was right: she was scamming me!

'Some guest house,' I remarked bitterly, my laugh scornful.

'What's the joke?' she demanded.

'You're a bloody liar!' I turned on her angrily. She trembled and backed away. I was glad I'd scared her. 'It's what you said it is: a boathouse, and an empty one at that. Why have you brought me here?'

'Take your hand off my arm!' she cried.

I tightened my grip. 'Are you Ceridwen?'

'Ceridwen?'

'You keep trolling us on Pictapost.'

'What? I do *not!* Let *go* of me!'

I put my hand over her mouth to muffle her screams and frogmarched her towards the boathouse, leaving my case on the sidewalk. The urge to chuck her into one of the boats and leave her there was becoming more appealing by the minute. Such a pity they'd be chained up without a chance of sending her out onto the lake.

'OW!' She'd bitten my hand. 'Bitch!'

For that, I slapped her hard and instantly regretted it. She staggered and fell back on the grass verge, clutching her cheek, her hair a mess and her expression full of hatred. My stuttered apology fell on deaf ears. She sprang up and lunged at me, nails poised to scratch. Defensively, I grabbed her wrists and dragged her towards the edge of the shore, ignoring her yells to let go. Seeing that no one had come running to investigate the racket, it was safe to assume she hadn't drawn any attention. There were four rowboats tucked under the pier chained together and without thinking any more of it I pushed her into one of them, her shrieks of anger ringing in the air. She scrambled to her feet and shook her fist, shouting obscenities. How she got out of the boat was her problem. I was wrong to shove her, but she'd started it.

'See you around,' I taunted her.

Without glancing back, I went to where I'd left my case and towed it towards the direction of the town centre. My mind turned to food again: a sandwich and hot drink would do; a light bite. There were a few cafés around to choose from.

On receiving the blow to my head, everything went black, and the world melted into darkness.

Thirteen
Cherry

'He's in a pretty bad way.'

The poor lad was clearly unwell. The first aid training course at my last school came to my rescue and I was relieved on examining his pulse to find he had a strong heartbeat. His forehead, on the other hand, was hot and clammy, a bad sign.

'Bloody hell, Tash!' Suki was shocked. 'What on earth did you hit him with?'

We were all horrified at the situation. A quaking and sobbing Tasha, incapable of speech, hovered outside the door to the boathouse, her hands covering her mouth. We'd found her sheltering from the snow in the doorway of Boots, shivering and distressed, and on hearing her garbled tale, brought her back to the boathouse to find this mysterious boy she said she'd killed. We found out much later she'd used a large stone, not realising how hard she'd hit him, and was scared at how easily he'd fallen down. We speculated he must have recovered enough to find his own way into the boathouse for shelter.

Rahma, also close to shedding the waterworks, was hugging her, trying to soothe her and saying, 'He'll be OK, Tasha,' without much conviction.

After I'd touched the boy's forehead, Suki gave me a bottle of hand sanitiser she kept in her bag and insisted I rubbed some of it into my palms.

'I'll call an ambulance,' she said.

'Help's on its way,' I told the lad, rubbing his hand. 'Hang in there. They won't be long.'

I hope.

'We should leg it,' I said to the others. 'If the police turn up an' all…'

Tasha was in no state to face an interrogation and we weren't up for any awkward questioning, either. We'd be in a whole heap of crap if the police traced us. Why should we be excluded and have our lives ruined because Tasha had been a prize idiot? My own plans for the future were vague, but Rahma had ambitions to go to Cambridge to train for medicine, Suki to the Sorbonne, and Tasha had been told if she kept her head down and worked hard she'd have the chance to get to university for some course or other. As a result, and pushing aside our mutual regret for leaving the poor lad at the boathouse, that's exactly what we did.

We sneaked back into school the same way we'd crept out, nearly getting caught by some Sixth Formers hanging around outside Oak House, drinks in their hands, enjoying a 'tea party' birthday celebration (Tasha testified she'd seen a couple of them dressed incognito in Tesco earlier buying wine and gin). Fortunately, they were so busy getting tanked up and enjoying themselves they took barely any notice of us.

We got back to Rowan House unscathed and the house mother's office was in darkness; Ragnarsson must have gone back to his own room in the main building.

Rahma collapsed on her bed and sighed thankfully. 'I'm desperate for a hot chocolate, I'm bloody freezing!'

We were all gasping for one; the problem was the kettle was in our common-room. Dare one of us sneak down and get it? We decided we'd taken enough risks for one night.

'There's half a bottle of rum left in the back of my knicker drawer,' said Suki. 'That'll warm us up and help us sleep.'

Rahma gave that the thumbs up. Tasha sat dazed on the edge of her bed, not knowing what to do.

'Let's get her into bed,' said Rahma.

Between us we undressed her, helped her into her pyjamas and dressing-gown, and tucked her into bed. Suki poured the drinks into our mugs and downed hers in one. Tasha held her mug and stared into space.

'Drink up, Tash,' I coaxed, 'it'll help calm you down.'

Eventually, she drained the mug and we waited for her to fall asleep, keeping our conversation general: volleyball, hockey, Rahma's place in the football team, successfully staying off the subject of the mystery boy. We planned to question Tasha the next day, hoping she'd be in a better frame of mind and willing to give us more details. I got into bed and heard my phone buzz: a Whatsapp from Suki to me and Rahma, hoping the ambulance had found the boy and that he was safe in hospital.

I sent Danny a message. 'Something awful's happened. I'll tell you tomorrow.'

Not being in the mood for a long natter, I signed off.

Thanks to the boy in the boathouse weighing heavily on my mind, I slept badly that night and woke up the next day massively hung over on lack of kip. He'd been really poorly and it was awful that, under the circumstances, we'd had to leave him. I prayed and prayed the ambulance had found him and he was safely getting treatment. First chance I got I planned to ring around the local hospitals to see if anyone matching his age and description had been taken to hospital. Remorse and empathy drew me to him somehow and I needed to find out how he was.

The enormity of what Tasha had done kicked in and she lost it. We had a hard job keeping her calm and preventing her from going to Panesar to confess and dropping all four of us in the shit. Rahma called the two main hospitals in the area that took emergency patients and if he had been taken to either of them, they weren't giving much away. We also surfed the internet and Twitter and trawled through local bulletins on the telly for news of a boy found bludgeoned in the Coniston boathouse.

'Nothing,' said Rahma, turning her iPad off. 'Not even on local radio.'

The news gradually filtered through on the school jungle drums: a man in Tesco told one of our teachers that he'd heard a boy found in the boathouse in the early hours had been taken to the Royal Kendal Hospital, where I'd had my ankle x-rayed. The teacher had told another teacher outside a classroom between lessons and the conversation had been overheard by a girl on her way back to class from the toilets. The exaggerated tale reached our form's ears that evening in the common-room. Clarissa Cleverly came running in shouting, 'Hey, have you heard? A boy's body was found in the boathouse last night! He was stabbed to death!'

'Stabbed?'

'That's awful!'

'Who'd do such a horrible thing?'

'Was it a gang?'

'The police are investigating.'

Luckily, Tasha's cries of, 'It's not true!' weren't heard in the commotion and we steered her out of the common-room and to our room to prevent her from saying anything else incriminating. Clarissa had turned on the telly for the local news and I heard a yell of, 'Hey! They're interviewing a detective!'

There'd been little chance to speak to Tasha all day. Classes kept getting in the way and if we tried to broach the subject she clammed up. Now we sat her down on her bed and Suki said, 'Right, Tasha, you've had hours to get your story straight. Come clean now! What happened last night? Did he try and assault you? You must have had a good reason for bashing him on the bonce.'

Haltingly, stutteringly, Tasha told us about the boy in the boathouse.

'He'd come to see *me*?' I said, stunned.

'Yeah. He said it was a surprise.' With the story out in the open, Tasha, a bit calmer, cleared her throat and continued. 'He said you and him were pen-pals.'

'It's news to me.'

Tasha was wringing her hands. 'You are, sort of, and I recognised him.'

'Did you?'

'From your Pictapost account.'

I raised my eyebrows.

'He's American.'

'Oh.' Was it Danny? No, Danny's hair was practically black whereas that boy's hair had been a lighter brown. Speaking of Danny, why hadn't he messaged me? If I was honest, I hadn't had the opportunity to ponder on that much because of other things going on.

I sat on my bed and puffed out my cheeks, trying to calm my nerves. 'Did you ask his name?'

'No. I'm certain it's not that lad you're hooked on now, though. It's not Danny.'

I was disappointed and relieved. 'Why do you reckon this other lad's on my Pictapost list?'

'He reminded me of a picture you showed us of a lad you were talking to on there; you were really into him and showed us lots of photos. Oh, what was his name?'

A light switched on in my brain. 'Hey! Do you think...is it Adam?'

'Adam?' chorused Rahma and Suki.

'Yeah, he was American. He shared that post of me in my uniform and had his account deleted. The man on the news called him Boy A – A for Adam?'

'Oh, yeah,' said Suki, nodding. 'Except why come all the way from America to see you?'

'Wait, isn't he the one you said was at the school down south, Cherry?' queried Rahma.

'Yeah, he was, in Suffolk.' Now that I was really into Danny, Adam had easily faded from my memory and I tried to visualise him. I vaguely recalled his hair colour and that was it. It was such a pity what had happened to our brief online fling that had led me to Danny. 'I didn't recognise him last night, though.'

And yet…

'Now I come to think of it, Cherry,' Tasha piped up, 'I'm certain it was him. He said he lived in the UK.'

'Did he say where?'

'In the south of England, I think.'

I frowned at her. Adam had told me he was at school in Suffolk.

'If you have no photos left of Adam, Cherry, you have to find out if it's him,' said Suki.

'Oh, yeah, and how do I do that?'

If I downloaded an app to retrieve Adam's deleted images…

'Visit him at the hospital, dumdum; find out what he remembers,' Tasha winced and Suki continued, 'for *her* sake.'

'They won't let me see him, I'm not a relative; and that's always supposing he hasn't been moved to a Suffolk hospital, if it *is* Adam.'

'Tell them you're his cousin,' Rahma suggested.

'They won't fall for that. I'm not American.'

'I'm Kenyan and I have a Danish cousin.'

'Really?'

'Yes. She was born and still lives in Roskilde.'

'You have a good imagination, Cherry,' said Suki encouragingly. 'You'll think up a story.'

I tutted. They were determined I was going and there'd be no getting out of it. Also, Suki was right: both Tasha and I needed answers from this boy.

'Tasha hasn't explained why she walloped him,' stated Suki. 'Come on, Tash, why did you?'

'I – I…' Tasha stammered, 'I – it was...'

'It was what?'

'Tagging Cherry's photos.'

I blushed. 'If it *was* him, it was no excuse to belt him, Tash.'

'He pushed me into one of the boats.'

'Why?'

'I bit him on the hand.'

'You did what?'

'He hit me back.'

'He *hit* you?'

'He accused me of trolling you and I got angry; and he pushed me in the boat...'

'*Have* you been trolling?' My mind turned again to Ceridwen. 'Did he mention the name "Ceridwen"?'

Tasha was crying now. 'I dunno, Cherry, it's all a blur. I haven't been trolling anyone, honest. I binned Pictapost since...' She trailed off.

I huffed. 'I'll have to go and see him at the weekend.'

'Go tomorrow,' said Rahma. 'Strike while the iron's hot. You're right, if they haven't already, it's possible they'll send him back to a hospital near where he lives or back to the States if he has come over from there.'

'Tomorrow?'

'It's half-day Wednesday. Have you forgotten the monthly staff meeting?'

I had. Half-day Wednesday afternoons were longed-for lazy hours spent doing what we wanted, within reason, and we were allowed to change out of uniform. The problem was, we had to stay in school until the end of the official working day. The prefects saw to that.

'It's always harder to get out during the day,' said Suki. 'The drill's the same: escape using the usual method, through the fence at the end of the field. Relax; we'll cover for you.'

'I'll be seen in daylight by the security cameras,' I said.

'Leave that to me,' said Rahma.

'How?'

She tapped her nose. 'You'll find out. Listen, Cherry, you need to put your mind at rest, find out why he came to see you.'

'I'll go with you, Cherry,' declared Tasha.

'No, Tash,' said Suki. 'It'll be harder covering for both of you and what if he recognises you?'

'What's the number of the bus I get? Karen took me there in the car after I sprained my ankle in hockey, and the hospital's an hour away.'

Suki got out her phone and began to surf the internet for bus and train times. Tasha said, 'It's forty minutes on the train to Kendal from Helton and there you catch the number fourteen to the hospital. It stops right outside. I went there for – for psych appointments on the bus occasionally.' She went red and turned away.

Suki cleared her throat. 'I'll find out when visiting is.'

It was all planned. Visiting was between two and four in the afternoon and six and eight in the evening. The bus from Kendal Station to the hospital ran every twenty minutes; the problem was the Helton to Kendal train ran once a day at twelve-thirty and I'd have to get the three-thirty back.

'I'll have to wait ages before visiting!' I said gloomily. 'What'll I do until then?'

'Have your lunch in the hospital café,' suggested Rahma. 'Eat a decent meal for once. You won't miss the muck they serve here, that's for sure.'

'Oh, yeah? I have to pay for my own scran?' I joked.

'Oh, for Chrissake, I'll lend you some dosh if you're that hard up!' said Suki impatiently.

'I'm kidding; I think I can afford it.' At least Greg gave me a decent amount of pocket money each month. 'I begrudge paying for it, that's all. We get it for nothing here.'

'Not quite for nothing, sweetie, our school fees pay for it, albeit on the cheap.'

Getting back to school was going to be a pain; if I left the hospital at half-past two, fingers crossed I'd get back for supper. I had no intention of staying long, just find out who the mystery boy was, what he knew of that fateful evening, and leave.

Fourteen
Adam

Waking up to an absolute mother of a headache confirmed I was alive. I tried to focus, not that I saw much. It was cold, draughty and dark and a persistent, irritating, knocking noise stabbed my ears. I sat up and rubbed the back of my throbbing head. There was a sticky substance on my fingers: blood. I had no idea how I'd got here, how long I'd been here, and I needed strong painkillers.

Flashes of memory: Cherry; Helton; a boathouse; a weird girl saying she went to Cherry's school, her biting my hand, and me pushing her into a boat. Surely she'd been the one who'd assaulted me? I sat up carefully and reached over to the chair for my jeans, finding my wallet and phone in the pocket. At least I hadn't been mugged.

It was all slowly flooding back to me and I relived the events that had brought me to the hospital.

What a massive mistake coming to Helton! I had to get out of this crazy town. Where the hell was my trolley case? Unable to see a thing, I shone my phone light and looked around. I was inside the boathouse, on the wooden walkway, and realised the knocks were coming from a couple of rowboats clashing into one another on the water next to me. The ripples showed how windy it was and there was also a blizzard raging outside.

My case was nowhere to be seen. Was it outside? Had that girl taken it? Good luck to her if she tried to open it: it was padlocked and had nothing more than my overnight stuff inside. I had a vague memory of seeing stars. She must have dragged me into the boathouse, that slip of a thing. I had to think of getting out of here, finding my belongings and going home to Mom and Dad.

I wobbled to a standing position, as though my legs had a problem supporting my body. I stumbled towards the door that led to the lake shoreline and turned the handle. Suddenly, the world began to spin and I was falling backwards, the girl's words ringing in my head, 'I've got a message from Cherry. She said to sod off and die!'

They kept me in hospital for three days; on top of the injury to my head I also had the flu, therefore accounting for my symptoms on the journey up to Helton. Having concussion and four stitches in my head added to my wretchedness and it was lucky the CT scan showed no lasting damage. I was declared unfit to go back to school and having no clue what kind of shit I'd be in on my return, it was probably a good idea I stayed away. The texts and Whatsapp messages I received from Aziz, Carlton-Greene, and, surprisingly, Petrov, first enquiring where I was and had I left, and finally telling me they'd found out what had occurred and were glad I was safe, gave no indication on the general mood at school to my absence. I was glad to hear from them and pleased that they'd been in touch.

Waking up in the Royal Kendal Hospital had been a shock and the doctor told me where I'd been found. The whole sorry episode was relayed in the news and the papers, where I was nicknamed Boy A due to being fifteen. My parents had been told what had happened and the police had paid a visit. I lied to them, claiming my mind was blank. I aimed to keep Cherry's name out of it, not to protect her, but to avoid looking stupid for getting my ass into such a dumb situation. My brain was foggy on the finer details of my attacker's exact description: red hair and pretty, not very tall, wearing a black coat, at least I thought it was black. Her words: 'I've got a message from Cherry. She said to sod off and die!' was all that goaded my mind. Surely that was a lie if Cherry had no knowledge of me being there?

Unless the girl had texted her somehow without my noticing, telling her I was in Helton and Cherry had guessed my identity by her description.

Thanks to the flu and the concussion, I struggled to concentrate on much, even my phone, not bothering to read any messages. I'd taken one call from Mom. A mixture of pride and lack of trust prevented me from messaging Cherry. My fever worsened and I began to imagine all sorts, developing a strong resentment against Cherry that was in danger of taking over my reasoning. She hadn't messaged me for days, reinforcing my suspicions she'd discovered I'd been playing her and I was convinced she'd told that girl to see me off.

The student nurse, a plump, attractive girl, her long blonde hair tied in a bun on top of her head, wandered across to my bed to collect my lunch food tray on the second day of my stay in the ward and shook her head at my small portion of untouched and now stone cold chicken soup.

'What's wrong with that?' she said, clearly affronted by the fact I hadn't eaten it.

'Sorry. I can't stomach it.'

'You have to eat. I'll bring you a Build Up drink and a cup of tea.'

I was unimpressed. 'That Build Up is disgusting, I'll throw it back up, and no offence, your tea is like dishwater.' I reached for the jug of water and poured some into the plastic glass.

She laughed. 'Now, Adam, you need to get your strength back and that means you have to try and eat and drink properly.'

'Aren't you supposed to feed a cold and starve a fever?'

'That's a myth. You can eat small amounts, enough to keep your strength up, and the Build Up drinks will give you nutrition. Oh, by the way, I nearly forgot,' she picked up the tray, 'you had a visitor.'

'What?'

'We only allow relatives on this ward and seeing you're not from round here we assumed you have no family in Kendal.' I confirmed she was right. 'Reception rang and said there was a girl...'

'A girl?' I sat up quickly and wished I hadn't; my head span and I flopped back on the pillow. 'What was her name? What did…?'

'Sorry, Adam, Sister told Reception to send her away.'

Bloody Sister! Cherry's school was in this neck of the woods. Was it her, come to apologise for that other girl? Perhaps it was my assailant. The mystery was killing me and the cogs in my brain were on overdrive, to the point where I ended up refusing more food.

***

The next day I was a bit better and having suffered more dishwater tea, I acknowledged Scott and Dean's messages, telling them I was ill, without the sordid details of what had happened; that was a conversation for a later date. I also reported and blocked Ceridwen for one of her 'you're a fake' comments. Mom arrived in the late afternoon and instead of dressing, I stayed in my pyjamas and wrapped my dressing-gown snugly around my body.

'Let's go home,' said Mom, pecking me on the cheek and picking up my bag.

I was offered a wheelchair to be chauffeured to Mom's car and declined, preferring to walk. I was slow and wobbly on my legs, not out of place wandering the hospital corridors in my sleeping gear. We ambled along, Mom's arm linked through mine. We discussed the food and how busy the hospital was, steering clear of the subject of the accident, school and Dad. I was grateful for the long pauses that gave me the opportunity to scan passers-by to see if I could spot the very person I hoped had tried to visit me. Of course, I was disappointed and left Kendal, fretting I'd missed my chance of seeing her.

We arrived back at the air force base around six and I was packed off to bed carrying a hot water bottle and a steaming mug of honey and lemon. Dad was working the late shift at the base.

'How is he?' I said.

'He's working hard,' Mom told me curtly. I said no more. Possibly they'd had words over what he was planning to say to me once I was fit enough to stand a rocket up my ass.

I woke to the light of the hall landing and saw Dad creeping round my room in T-shirt and shorts, trying to quietly put my clothing in my drawers. Mom had insisted on washing the stuff in my weekend case. He noticed me peering at him over my duvet.

'Sorry for waking you, son. It's nearly nine o'clock. You've been asleep for five hours. How do you feel?' He put his hand on my forehead. 'Hmm, you're a bit clammy. I'll fetch you Paracetamol and another honey and lemon drink. This one's gone cold.'

I'd hardly touched the contents. He picked up my mug and I marvelled at how calm he was acting, considering I'd gone AWOL to see a girl I'd met on social media and caused him and Mom a whole heap of grief.

'No, just water, please. Dad?' He turned to me. 'Sorry,' I said falteringly.

He smiled encouragingly. 'We'll work it out, champ.'

He left the room, coming back five minutes later carrying a glass of water and two Paracetamol tablets. I had my phone in my hand, reading a message from Cherry, asking why she hadn't heard from me and spinning me a story of a mystery boy she and her pals had found injured in the boathouse near her school. She'd visited the boy because she was concerned for him.

That girl *had* lied and Cherry *had* visited me! My emotions soared. Had she recognised the real me and did part of her still care?

'I'll take that, boy,' said Dad, taking the phone out of my hand and snapping shut the cover. 'Your buddies can wait. Take your tablets.'

He waited for me to take the tablets and left me alone, carrying my phone. My confused and fevered mind went through the events in Helton, trying to fathom them out. What if Cherry *had* said to sod off and die?

I had strange dreams that night. All sorts of people were coming at me: Cherry, that girl, Petrov, Aziz, all merging together and morphing into a nightmare that resulted in me screaming.

A cold cloth landed on my forehead.

'He's burning up!' Mom's distress broke in to my nightmare. I opened my eyes to see her smoothing my damp hair away from my hot skin.

'Is Dr Henry coming, Mom?'

'He's on his way.' That was Dad. 'Hell, he's really sick, honey! Hey!' Mom jumped aside and Dad dragged me over the side of the bed to help me find the bucket. I'd clearly missed it on another occasion judging by the baking soda sprinkled on the carpet, Mom's usual remedy to clear up puke. I tucked my legs up to try and relieve the pain in my stomach.

Shortly, the base doctor was resting a stethoscope against my chest and back, feeling my pulse and pressing his hands on my stomach. Outside, I heard muffled words and Mom and Dad came back in, Mom using the back of her hand to wipe away tears. What was going on?

I croaked, 'Mom, what's wrong? Am I – am I dying?'

Dad laughed. 'No! Your mom's relieved, is all.'

'What did the doctor say?'

'The flu's been making you sick and the retching sore, that's all. It won't last long. Doc Henry thinks you should've stayed in hospital a bit longer, but we'll take care of you and call him again if we need to. He reckons you'll live,' he added, winking.

I managed to joke, 'I'll remind you of that if I die.'

I took the anti-sickness pill Dr Henry prescribed for the vomiting and at last drifted off to sleep, waking to daylight outside, my bedside clock showing five-past eight. I rolled over and Mom was sleeping next to me, on top of the bed, hidden under a duvet.

'Mom.' I shook her slightly and she was suddenly awake.

'Adam. How are you?'

'Better.' My headache had gone for one thing. 'I think I slept. Have you been here all night?'

'Yes.' She glanced at her watch. 'You passed out around eleven last night.'

'You'll be late for work.'

'I'm not going in today. I can work from home.' She yawned, ran her fingers through her long hair and pulled up into a sitting position.

'I'm really thirsty, Mom.'

'I'm not surprised,' she said. 'You're dehydrated. I'll fetch you some water. Dr Henry says that's all you can have for now and you have to take it easy.'

She brought a jug of water and ice, placed that and a glass next to my bed and went to have a shower. I was glad the water stayed down and, washed out, I fell asleep again. A few hours later, I heard the front door slam and feet pounding up the stairs. Dad walked in, dressed in uniform and seeing that I was awake came straight over to the bed.

'How are you, pal?'

'A bit better, thanks, Dad. I drank some water and it stayed down.'

'Good. Anyway, we'll need to discuss all this in the near future, you know…'

I nodded.

'Not now; later.'

I was fully prepared for the grilling that awaited me. Dad's bark was worse than his bite and whatever rant was to come would be harsh and short-lived.

'Can I have my phone, Dad, to text Scott and Dean?'

Cherry will have to wait.

'Don't stay on long, Adam,' said Dad, handing it over reluctantly. 'You need more rest.'

There was plenty of charge left in the battery and I tapped on Pictapost. There were messages from Scott and Dean asking how I was and I told them what had been going on. There were more trolling comments and messages from another Ceridwen account to sort out, and finally Cherry's frantic questions: *Where are you? What's the matter? Are you ghosting me?* The last message was sent an hour ago and there was nothing said of the 'mystery boy'. So what, I was sick and couldn't give a damn. Now I was reminded of it and saw Cherry's message, my mind in turmoil. My confidence in this online romance had been rocked. Was Cherry the real deal? What if *she* was out to scam *me*?

Possibly the bang on my head had robbed me of all sense and reasoning and convinced me it had been no accident I'd bumped into that girl; I was beginning to believe Cherry had told her to pass on that message, in spite of her not being aware I was in Helton. The attack had been real enough and showed the hazard of falling for a stranger online. It was all a fantasy, not real love at all, and she hadn't fallen for the real me, she'd fallen for a fake, for Danny.

I blew a kiss at my favourite image of her, the one in her school uniform, trying to persuade myself to walk away, forget her. Perhaps that was sensible and I ought to move on.

Mom came up half an hour later bearing a tray of food and a fresh glass of water.

'Fancy some chicken soup?'

Groaning, I sat up and she put the tray on my lap. The smell of the soup was overwhelmingly repulsive.

'Urgh, it's what they tried to force down my throat in the hospital! Why do they always give chicken soup to sick people? I'd rather be ill.'

'It's traditional and supposed to be really good for you. Eat what you can.'

I dipped my spoon in the soup and took a few sips, giving up at the first sign of nausea.

A Pictapost notification came through on my phone and Mom picked it up and handed it to me.

I shook my head. Sleep was more important to me right now. 'It's probably a message from Scott. I can call him later.'

Fifteen
Cherry

'I was told to bugger off,' I informed them gloomily. 'I'm not a relative, see. The crabby old cow on the reception desk was working on her own and there were a crowd of people waiting to be seen, her phone was ringing and ringing and she was in a right ratty mood. I tried to tell her I was his cousin and she said if the Sister refused to let me in that was that. I didn't dare push it, there were police hanging round, that's why I got out of there sharpish.'

I was tired and hacked off. What a wasted journey it had been, going all that way and not being allowed to see him! Plus the hospital café was closed for redecorating; all that was on offer were sandwiches and crisps at the shop and I decided to get a bite at the train station. The boring bus and train journey over, I'd arrived back at Helton at ten-past four, expecting a grim welcoming committee. Surely the staff meeting was over by now and I'd been missed, despite the others promising they'd do their best to cover for me.

Scrambling through the gap in the fence, my mind turned to Rahma's bold plan to fiddle the security cameras and whether she'd succeeded. I received a nasty shock seeing her and a group of ten other sporty types, prefects among them, jogging around the pitch. The wintry climate had meant hockey and football fixtures were cancelled, forcing the sporty brigade to use the gym and to go running in calmer weather, Rahma included.

The joggers came to a surprised halt at my sudden, stumbling entrance through the hedge, their barrage of questions unexpectedly and dramatically interrupted by Rahma.

'OW! Ooooh! It hurts!'

She screamed and fell on the grass, clutching her calf in mock-agony and complaining of horrendous cramp.

'*Ooooooooh!*'

Grateful for Rahma's theatrics, I seized my opportunity and ducked back into the hedge out of sight, dying to laugh at her Oscar-winning performance. The others helped her to stand and guided her back to the school building. I waited until they were a safe distance away then ventured back out from the hedge and texted to Suki and Tasha, 'I'm back.'

No one else challenged me on my way to the common-room. I'd found a café at Kendal Station that sold bacon and tomato baguettes and had coffee on the train, now I was hungry again and supper was an hour away. One of the girls had had a birthday recently and I hoped there was cake left in the kitchen fridge. I was also thirsty and paying no attention to the handful of girls gossiping over coffee, I opened the fridge door, disappointed to find no cake and a drop of lemonade left. Swigging the last of it, I turned my attention to the window and saw Mr Ragnarsson by the gate talking to a man next to a white van, the word *Securio*, a mobile number and email address written on the side.

Suki's voice broke into my thoughts. 'Clarissa ate the last of the cake, the greedy cow.' I chucked the empty lemonade bottle in the recycling bin. 'Nice stroll, Cherry-chan?' she enquired in a too-loud, too-obvious tone.

'Yes, thanks.' I feigned a shiver and added, 'Brrr, it's a bit chilly out there! I'd love a hot drink to warm me up and I'm starving.'

'Good idea,' said Suki. 'You had such a long walk! I'll make you a hot chocolate and my papa sent two tins of biscuits, posh ones from Fortnum and Mason. I haven't taken them to the common-room to share yet...'

She winked and nodded her head towards the door. Grinning, I took the hint and the first thing I did in our room was take off my coat, kick off my boots, chuck my bag on the bed and collapse in one of the chairs. The biscuit tin and mug of hot chocolate were placed on the table in front of me and we were expecting Rahma and Tasha any minute.

Rahma came in, fresh from a shower, and I clapped. Tasha entered and she and Suki demanded an explanation.

'Clever darling!' said Suki to Rahma approvingly.

'And did you fiddle the CCTV?' I said to Rahma, expecting her to say no.

'I did!' She laughed. 'It was simple! The computer monitor is in the gatehouse and all the cables run along the wall by the fence. I unplugged one of them and legged it out of there.'

I was shocked that Rahma, a stickler for rules, had considered doing such an outrageous thing. Suki and Tasha giggled. I was impressed. 'How did you know the right cable to unplug, and how did you do it?'

'My home in Kenya has a similar security system to the Manor's and the cable thing was a guess. Our house has cameras everywhere. There's one main cable the individual cables feed into. I reckoned if I unplugged the wrong one it'll keep the gatehouse staff occupied trying to figure out what the problem was and they won't take much notice of the other cameras. I went round the back and waited for one of the men to go on his break and the other one was speaking to the supermarket delivery driver at the barrier. I took a big risk, sneaked in the back door, tugged at a cable and ran out again. It took me less than a minute.'

'Rahma! You legend! That's why the security van is out in the drive!'

'More than likely.'

'I hope no one saw you,' said Tasha.

'No fear. I was really careful. Right,' Rahma selected a biscuit, 'spill the beans, Cherry. What happened in Kendal?'

I was on my fifth chocolate biscuit by the time I finished my story.

'Did you find out his name at least?' enquired Suki, on her third pistachio, her favourite. Tasha had refused her share. She was pale and nervous and had apparently eaten very little breakfast and lunch.

'No.'

'That's a nuisance,' observed Rahma.

'What now?' said Tasha.

I shook my head. 'Nothing, I suppose. There's not much more we can do.'

'The thing is,' said Tasha apprehensively, 'the police have been all over Helton, interviewing people, and it said in the paper they're looking for a red-head!'

'Really?'

'Yes; and there aren't that many red-haired girls in Helton!'

'We've already told you, Tash!' said Rahma irritably. 'You're not a red-head, you daft mare, you have red and blonde highlights. There's a big difference.'

'Do what we told you to do this morning,' said Suki. 'At your next appointment get your hairdresser to dye your hair another colour. You'd suit green.'

Tasha ignored the joke and said, 'Won't that seem a bit suspicious?'

'What do you mean?'

'People implying I covered the red to avoid being caught out.'

We rolled our eyes at her.

'Oh, for God's sake, Tash!' cried Rahma. 'You're panicking for no reason!'

Tasha refused to budge from the idea that any moment the police might come knocking and she'd be carted off to the cells. Her panic nearly reached boiling point the next day; a police car had been spotted in the drive and our year tutor announced a couple of detectives were visiting each class to interview everyone. Tasha fainted and had to be taken to the san. Matron told her to lie down on the bed and had little sympathy for her on hearing from Rahma that she'd hardly eaten a thing for two days.

'If only they knew!' muttered Suki to Rahma and me.

The door to the Chemistry lab opened and the two detectives, a man and a woman, wearing smart outfits and ID badges on their police lanyards, entered. Judging by his expression, Mr Scarfe, the Chemistry teacher, was clearly unimpressed by the disruption to the class.

Jenny was approximately six feet in height and slim in her black trousers, white blouse and black jacket; her colleague, Anthony, was tall and hunky. We nudged one another and whistled appreciatively.

'That'll do, you lot!' snapped Mr Scarfe. 'Shut up and listen. The earlier this nonsense is over the better.'

'It's not nonsense, Mr Scarfe,' said Anthony coldly. 'A boy was attacked and he identified a schoolgirl, around the age of these girls, being the assailant.'

'From this school?' said Mr Scarfe.

'That's what we're trying to ascertain,' said Jenny.

I shifted in my seat, relieved for Tasha she was absent from class to hear what Jenny was saying. The police must be onto something. Had the boy identified Tasha's Helton Manor uniform somehow, even though she'd been cocooned in her hooded coat against the cold and the snow? We were informed a few Helton Manor girls had been seen in town when the incident was said to have occurred and a couple of people had witnessed one girl chatting to a boy matching his description. The police had examined the CCTV recordings at the main gate and found parts of the recording missing. Phew! Not that it mattered: Tasha had left the school using the illegal method through the fence.

'Was anyone in your class out that evening?' Jenny questioned us. 'At around five?'

'Was she in uniform?'

'Unfortunately, the boy was unsure what she was wearing,' said Jenny. I puffed out my cheeks silently. That let Tasha off the hook – for now.

'No girl is allowed out alone in the evening from Years Seven to Eleven unless accompanied by a Sixth Former or teacher, especially in the winter,' Mr Scarfe informed her. 'At the weekend they can go out in pairs and groups. We have a duty of care and responsibility to keep them safe from some of the dodgier characters in this town. It's very unlikely any girl from *this* year was out on that day in such bad weather. Now, if that's all, I have a lesson to teach.'

Jenny and Anthony exchanged glances and we suppressed laughter. The damaged fence was common knowledge throughout the school population and that included the teachers. One by one, we swore blind we hadn't been out that evening and twenty minutes later Mr Scarfe closed the door behind the coppers, tutting and shaking his head.

'That's that,' he said grumpily to the class, 'and now most of the lesson's gone, put your textbooks away and we'll have a shout-out test.'

Suki sent Tasha a text to tell her how the police visit had gone, enabling Tasha to drag her backside to the dining-hall and find some appetite for sausage and mash. Half an hour later, there was a special assembly where Panesar told us the police had gone away, satisfied a Helton Manor girl hadn't been involved in the attack on the boy and they were visiting other schools nearby.

On her way out of the assembly hall, Rahma was taken to one side by our year tutor. 'Come along, please, Rahma, Miss Panesar is waiting for you in her office.'

'Yes, sir,' she murmured, glancing over her shoulder at us.

'What's that about?' whispered Suki to me.

'Dunno.'

'Hurry up, you two,' one of the prefects butted in, guiding us out of the room. 'You're holding everyone up.'

We soon found out why the year tutor had swept Rahma away. She was late for prep and apologised to the teacher on duty. She'd been crying and paid little attention to her work. Afterwards, we went to the common-room for tea and biscuits and she took us to a corner away from nosey parkers.

'What is it, Rahma?' wondered Tasha.

'One of the cameras caught me sneaking round the back of the gatehouse.'

Her hand trembling, Rahma put her tea on the table and broke the stunned silence by adding, 'No one saw me pull the wire, they have no proof it was me. So going back to the camera, Panesar interrogated me and I had to invent a story.'

'I hope it was convincing,' said Suki worriedly. She was very fond of Rahma and was furious at the idea of her being punished over the cable. Tasha and me were also anxious; Rahma had an unblemished record at the school.

'Erm,' Rahma bit her lip, 'I told her I'd gone to meet a boy round the back of the gatehouse for a kiss and cuddle!'

Suki shrieked loudly at this and immediately clamped her hand over her mouth.

'Did Panesar swallow that? She must have gone mental!'

'She was livid,' admitted Rahma. 'She wanted his name, of course, where he lived, where we'd met. Obvs I refused to tell her 'cos he doesn't exist and said he blew me out. She's going to ground me for the rest of this term and all of next and is phoning my parents right now.'

'Oh, Rahma-chan!' cried Suki. I grabbed Rahma's hands and Suki and Tasha hugged her. 'Your dad will have a fit!'

'There's nothing else for it,' I said gloomily. 'I'll have to go to Panesar and own up.'

'Be sensible, Cherry!' said Rahma. 'You'll get us all into deep doo-doos and how will you feel if Tasha gets carted off to jail?'

Tasha nearly choked on her tea. 'Rahma!'

'I was joking, Tash!'

'Rahma's right, Cherry,' said Suki. 'We're all implicated in this. We pushed you into breaking the rules to visit the lad. Best keep your trap shut.'

'It's no good. This is my fault! I really am sorry, Rahma.'

'Don't sweat it, Cherry. It was my idea,' said Rahma, her smile weak. She spent the rest of the evening concentrating on the telly and not saying much, apart from 'goodnight' to us up in our room.

Knowing the police had gone and weren't likely to come back nearly drove Tasha to distraction. Her relief was all-consuming and she took to her bed early, claiming a bad headache. It took a few days for her to get back to her usual self.

The phone call Rahma received from her dad the next day left her in floods. 'I have a good mind to take you out of Helton Manor and have you educated at home!' Her mother also had plenty to say and persuaded him to change his mind. No surprise therefore Rahma promised not to see the fictitious boy again.

A strong rumour went round that the security repair man had found a cable running along the wall of the gatehouse had been frayed and he suspected mice of having a feast. Four of the cameras were out of action during Tasha's escapade to town and my journey to Kendal.

'That accounts for the missing recording,' said Tasha.

'Unbelievable!' Suki remarked. 'And no one noticed?'

'Obviously they did, that's why they called the repair man in,' said Rahma. 'They had to wait a few days for him to turn up 'cos his company is short of staff.' She sniffed. 'It means I went to all that trouble for nothing!' She winked at me. 'I hope you're grateful, Cherry Hill!'

I gave her a hug to show her I was.

Having escaped a summons for sneaking out in school hours through the hole in the fence, I was fairly certain I was in the clear. It was announced by Panesar, however, the poor fence was going to be replaced by a high concrete wall.

What did frighten me was what I heard on the news. The police were investigating reports of a girl attempting to visit Boy A in hospital. Now I appreciated Tasha's unease: if the woman on the information desk at the hospital had been requested to give a description, I could be in big, big trouble!

Sixteen
Adam

Recovery from the flu and concussion did nothing to stem my belief that Cherry had betrayed me, meaning I had two people to seek revenge on. She'd been messaging me a lot, desperate for me to get in touch. For good and obvious reasons, I was in no position to comply.

'Have I done anything wrong?' she typed.

'I'm sorry, baby,' I wrote, 'my phone hasn't been working properly. I had to get a new one.'

These days, that was one of my rare truths. The battery on my cell had become unreliable and Dad had advanced my Christmas money for me to get an upgrade. I'd noticed Cherry had unfriended me, obviously sick of waiting for me to write back, and I couldn't blame her, really; at least she hadn't blocked me.

A notification came through *can @cherryhillpie be your friend* and that sent my ego soaring.

'I'm an idiot for contacting you again,' she wrote.

'I'm glad you did.'

'I can't keep away from you, Danny. I love you.'

My stomach was doing somersaults. Was she being genuine and did I love her back? That was what I'd been pondering a lot lately and I concluded it was possibly more lust than love, fancying her, of course, and imagining one day kissing her, touching her and giving her my all. My emotions were in constant conflict.

I let my mind drift to Mom and Dad and our interview, where I again employed the same strategy of selective amnesia and blissful ignorance.

'There must have been a reason why you went all the way up to the Lake District,' Mom probed cynically.

'It's all a blank,' I insisted.

'What can I say to that?' she grumbled in disbelief.

'Dunno, Mom.'

I'd been to a small town in the north of England she'd never heard of and nearly got beaten to death. I hadn't done it on purpose and I had intended to return to The Priory afterwards. I think I did a fairly good job keeping my expression neutral.

'I love the bones of you, Adam,' she said, 'but I swear to God you're a complete mystery to me and your dad!'

Dad said, 'We're disappointed in you, boy. Still, the main thing is you're safe and we guess you've had enough punishment.'

'Yes, Dad.'

Astonishingly, I came out of the affair pretty unscathed. Later, I overheard him and Mom in the living-room.

'Thanks for not being hard on him, love,' said Mom.

I almost choked at his next words. 'I was all set on sending him to military school in the US. They're more regimented than the places over here. He's not getting enough discipline at that Priory; it's for your sake he's going back. I'm sorry, honey, if this happens again, I'll carry out my threat.'

Dad related his long phone call with Crane. I overheard the words 'psychologist' and 'cognitive behavioural therapy'.

'I refused his kind offer, of course. Adam doesn't need a shrink and they're not gonna exclude him. It doesn't count if he was on a weekend furlough, duty of care or not. One thing we did agree on, the boy's been punished enough and that's why I've listened to you, honey, and not said any more. The school won't have him back unless he's A1 fit.'

I guessed I had to count myself lucky they were letting me back at all.

I decided not to listen to any more and went to my room to read my Pictapost messages, four from Ceridwen (deleted) and three from Cherry, questioning why I hadn't been in touch. Twenty minutes later, Mom called me down to supper. At the table, Dad grudgingly gave me the money for the new phone. 'Call it an early Christmas present,' he said. I suspected Mom had persuaded him to hand over the cash.

'Thanks, Dad.'

I transferred all my apps, data and photos to it and put Cherry out of her misery: 'Hello, baby. I have a new phone.'

She wrote back almost immediately. 'Hello, stranger, you haven't gone off me, I see.'

'No, baby; of course I haven't gone off you. Why say that?' I hesitated. What if I brought up my visit to Helton, give her the chance to explain? 'I guessed maybe *you'd* gone off *me* 'cos you unfriended me, is all. The new phone isn't a lie, honest.'

'I hadn't heard from you, had I?' A pause. 'I should really have blocked you for good.'

'Why didn't you?'

'I love you.'

'That's great, baby.'

'Is that all you have to say?'

'Sorry, baby. I also love you.' *Not true, not really*. 'Send me a pic, a real sexy one.'

'Danny! How can I do that? I'm in school!'

'Please, baby. I won't share it. Your snaps are mine. No one else will see my queen's beautiful body.'

Half an hour later she sent the photo, her legs astride a chair in black lacy bra and panties and her finger seductively in her mouth. I licked my lips and sensed the familiar sign of pleasure. Whether I loved her or not, she was good enough to eat and right now, I had a yearning to do more than eat her. That was pic number twenty added to my collection.

She liked my 'WOW!' and exploding head emoji.

'And the mystery boy?' Boy A and my mysterious visitor to the hospital they were trying to trace were absent from national UK TV and radio, but plenty was said in the online Cumbrian press. Why had Cherry ignored that?

'No more news,' she informed me.

'Really? That's interesting.'

That began regular contact between us again. Every one of her messages was full of love, promises, the occasional raunchy photo, and Boy A was history.

Walking into the common-room shortly before supper, I was amazed to see a banner screaming WELCOME BACK ADAM and cheers and applause breaking out.

'Here he is!' I heard over the racket. An unexpected welcome party, plates of buffet food scattered around the common-room and bottles of lemonade, cola and juice.

Aziz was the first one to come over and fist pump. Carlton-Greene and some of the others patted me on the back; Petrov, standing by the window and blowing out vape smoke, merely nodded, his penetrating eyes boring into me, making my heart race uncomfortably.

Why are you always staring at me?

I laughed. 'Whose bright idea was this?'

'We're happy to see you're alive, fit and well,' said Aziz.

'It was all over the local news,' added Carlton-Greene. 'You're a celebrity.'

'How come? They kept my name out of the press.'

'We'll explain how we found out,' said Aziz. 'Get him a drink, Freddie.'

A plastic cup containing orange juice and gin was thrust in my hand. The bottles of liquor were stashed on the windowsill, safely hidden behind the curtain in case a teacher walked in. I sipped it, enjoying the warm glow it gave me.

'You're a celeb here, anyway,' added Carlton-Greene.

'We'd been wondering what had happened to you,' said Aziz, a glass of fruit juice in his hand. Petrov wasn't drinking at all. 'We hadn't heard you'd been excluded and thought you'd left. There were all sorts of rumours flying round and Crane held a special assembly to put us straight. He told us everything. We were also told if any of us went blabbing to the press and posted stuff on social media we'd be excluded on the spot. The school was accountable for our welfare yada, yada, yada. You can imagine the sort of thing.'

'For at least twenty minutes,' added Carlton-Green, 'the old windbag!'

'No one has blabbed, of course.' Petrov took one last puff of his vape. 'You're not worth getting excluded for, Fisher.'

'Glad to hear it,' I said, sipping more gin and orange and peering at him over my glass.

'Can you remember any of it, why you were there?' questioned Aziz. 'What do the police know?'

Stick to the same story I fed the police. 'No, everything's a blank. I think there was a girl...'

'A girl?'

Oh, bollocks.

The liquor had loosened my tongue and out came the story of the boathouse and the girl, leaving out the fact she went to Cherry's school. Petrov listened without comment and the familiar pangs of guilt engulfed me. It was his image Cherry saw on Pictapost, not mine, and my conscience kept reminding me of that.

'Aren't you hungry, Fisher?' Carlton-Greene nudged me, his mouth full of pork pie. I surveyed the plates of sandwiches, chicken legs, pies and other nibbles without much enthusiasm. The liquor had robbed me of my appetite. 'Go on,' he handed me a paper plate, 'we've gone to a lot of trouble putting on this spread and the least you can do is have a sausage roll.'

'You must have had a reason why you went to the place,' said Petrov, switching off his vape and leaving the window. He sat down next to me and rested his cheek on his hand. 'I bet it was to meet a girl, huh?'

I concentrated piling food on my plate and said nothing.

It's none of your damn business.

'I bet it was her on Pictapost,' chipped in Carlton-Greene slyly. My gaze remained locked on Petrov's, sending the hairs on the back of my neck on end. What did Carlton-Greene mean? 'That Cherry, she's up at school in Helton, isn't she? Be honest, now; you went to see her, you sly dog.'

I turned quickly to him. 'What makes you think that?'

'I recognised the uniform she was wearing in that pic Petrov tagged,' he explained and I sensed the blood draining from my face. 'My younger sister starts at Helton Manor next year. She sent me a Whatsapp a few days ago and a photo of her posing in her new school gear.'

'*Did* you go and see this Cherry?' said Aziz.

My unsteady hand reached for a cocktail sausage. 'I – I'm telling you, it's all a bit of a blur.'

I wished they'd shut up and change the subject.

'Hell, what was her Pictapost name?' said Carlton-Greene. 'Remind me, Fisher. I'll send her a message and invite her to our farm for a roll in the hay. We have a lovely big barn and no one would hear us.'

'Dream on, CG, you have no chance,' Petrov said scornfully. 'And the pigs will object.'

We all laughed and the subject was dropped when somebody fell off the sofa drunk.

Seventeen
Cherry

'Hello, stranger,' I wrote, asking myself for the millionth time why I hadn't blocked him entirely. 'You haven't gone off me, I see.' A mixture of irritation and joy coursed through my body.

'No, baby; of course I haven't,' he said. 'I guessed maybe *you'd* gone off *me* 'cos you unfriended me, is all. The new phone isn't a lie, honest.'

'I hadn't heard from you, had I? I should really have blocked you for good.'

'What's stopping you?'

'I love you.' Silence. 'Are you there?'

'That's great, baby.'

'Is that all you have to say?'

'Sorry, baby. I also love you.'

'I should think so!'

'Send me a pic, a real sexy one.'

I blushed. 'Danny! How can I do that at school?'

'Please, baby. I won't share it. Your snaps are mine. No one else will see my queen's beautiful body.'

Don't do it, Cherry.

Ignoring the warnings in my head, I sloped off to Rowan House unnoticed at break to change into my lacy black bra and knickers, dressed again, and went to the single bathroom at the end of the corridor to strip off to my undies and take at least twenty selfies, finally settling on one of me sitting astride a chair, my finger in my mouth. Unable to decide if I came across silly or seductive, I sent it, dressed, and speedily tidied up for History class.

Arranging my books on my desk, I questioned my wisdom sending that pic to Danny. I'd trusted Adam and look what had happened! I sniffed. There I was again, thinking about him. It was weird how the attack on that boy had brought him to mind and if it was him why had he come to see me?

None of it made sense.

I was also fretting over the girl they were trying to find – me – and my trip to see him in hospital. What if the woman at the information desk had given the police a description and I was recognised on the train and the bus? Thankfully, there were no fuzzy CCTV pictures of me at the stations on the local news.

'Relax, darling,' Suki said. 'It's all good. You weren't wearing your uniform and there are a million girls in Cumbria fitting your description. Those two coppers haven't been back and the school authorities believe you were here. There's no evidence to suggest otherwise.'

Nothing Suki, Rahma nor Tasha said helped my depressed mood. While Tasha was now persuaded that she was out of the frame for the assault, I dreaded a visit from the police and a summons to Panesar's office. At least Tasha had come out the other end of the sorry affair fairly unscathed, regardless of the fact she'd nearly killed the poor lad.

The teacher came in and I had to temporarily put aside my self-torment. My phone buzzed: another message from Ceridwen slagging off Danny, calling him a catfish, a fraud and a scammer, the usual trolling crap. What was the point in grassing her to the Pictapost moderators? All they ever did was to advise me to change my password and I'd done that a hundred times. I put my account to private again and also changed my username to @queencherrybaby, in honour of what Danny called me. Danny and the creeps approved, judging by the comments left on my posts.

After class, Suki came up to me and dragged me off to a corner of the corridor out of earshot from the other girls rushing to their next classes.

'Cherry-chan, it's OK!' she hissed, hugging me and showing me her phone. 'Rahma-chan found this online: the woman on the information desk at the hospital hardly remembered you, her phone kept ringing, and there was a queue of people there. You can chillax now!'

'Oh, Suki!'

Elation washed over me like a warm shower and I called myself all kinds of an idiot for panicking over nothing. I cried, and seeing it confirmed on the local evening news caused me to spiral even further into despair. The police hadn't been given a description of the visitor and had no information from the ward, either. The trail had gone cold and soon the school and the town began to forget. Not me: I kept praying the boy was on the mend.

'Look on the bright side,' said Rahma later, 'he's not dead, else we'd've heard.'

The school had other things on its mind: Christmas was coming. I was on pins to get home and see Mum, Tulip and my grandparents again. Mum had hinted that Greg liked to go away to his villa in Spain at Christmas. Good riddance. I'd visit my old haunts and see Precious and Suze. Rahma was going back to Kenya, Suki and her mum and dad were visiting her grandparents in Kyoto and Tasha was going home to London. Their excited yapping was a plague on my poor ears. A three week break from school appealed to everyone.

'We've got tickets to see a couple of shows in the West End and also *Cinderella* at our local theatre,' Tasha said cheerfully. 'My Auntie Serena is playing the wicked stepmother.'

Tasha's Auntie Serena was the well-known television actor, Serena Tomlinson, and Tasha had also met a lot of famous people, ignoring Clarissa Cleverley's continual claims of all the film stars from Hollywood she said she'd met.

'My grandparents are throwing a big party,' said Suki. 'It's an opportunity to dress up and introduce me to prospective future husbands.'

We all burst out laughing.

'It's hilarious!' Suki chortled. 'My *obaa-chan,* that's my grandmother, is very old-fashioned and thinks it's how it must be done. My *ojii-san,* that's my grandfather, keeps reminding her it's the twenty-first century. *Obaa-chan* invites some "suitable" boy's family and tries to match us. I did consider telling her I'm a lesbian, 'cept that'll send the poor dear to an early grave!'

We joined in her fit of mirth at this and Rahma said, 'Papa is very strict and is keen for me to marry his cousin's son. Jaali really is a lovely person. We've known each other for years, from toddlers actually, and our families are very close. We will also have a big gathering for Christmas and it's our turn to host his family. I love Jaali, except not in that way. You see, there is a slight problem.' Rahma's mouth twitched. 'Jaali *is* gay. He has a boyfriend at school! He came out to me last year and I'm glad for him.' She shook her head. 'But poor Jaali is expected to marry a girl and it won't be me.'

'I'd hate to be forced to marry a stranger,' I said.

'I'm not sure I'll get married at all,' said Tasha.

'Why not, Tasha-chan?' queried Suki. 'It's good to be married and have a family of your own, if you choose your own partner. I'm still on the hunt for mine,' she added, smirking. It was the worst kept secret in the school that Suki was no virgin. She was beautiful and seductive, and had half the young men in Helton at her feet. All the girls envied Suki.

'I fancy travelling first,' said Tasha, 'visit all the out-of-the-way places: Greenland, for instance.'

Rahma was amused. 'Why Greenland?'

'It's always appealed to me, somehow, to live in an igloo amongst the Inuit,' stated Tasha calmly.

We laughed. 'Hilarious! You won't last five minutes in an igloo!' cried Suki.

'I'd last five more than you!' retorted Tasha good-naturedly.

It was true: Suki loved her creature comforts and Rahma shivered at the prospect of holidaying in Greenland; she found the damp British climate bad enough. She wrapped her cardigan tightly round her and said, 'It's good to see you laugh again, Tash.'

It was, although I often caught the occasional hint of sadness and disapproval at the mention of Danny's name. Such a shame; we'd been getting on much better lately. I showed her, Suki and Rahma a selfie of me in a low-cut top revealing my ample cleavage I'd posted that morning and we had another of our arguments, running its usual course of her saying things I loathed and me getting the hump.

'You're inviting trouble posting that stuff, Cherry.'

'Danny likes it,' I informed her coldly.

'Of course he does!'

'What are you implying, Tasha?'

'Oh, there's no point lecturing you!'

'That's true enough,' Rahma butted in. 'Be told, will you, Tasha: it's none of your business what Cherry posts if she isn't caught doing it.'

'That's right,' I muttered and Suki nudged a miffed Tasha. The teacher entered the room and I hastily put my phone away.

For the rest of the day, I mooched around thoroughly pissed off and turned to Danny for comfort, thinking what a pity it was I had no real-life, in-the-flesh boyfriend to confide in. In spite of being this supposedly dare-I-say-it hot, attractive, sexy sixteen-year-old girl, I hadn't met a lad at home and in Helton worth knowing. Yeah, I got the winks, the nods and the whistles, usually from builders and losers, and what were they but idiot pervs and nobodies?

An end-of-term Christmas party, to which the boys from a local boys' boarding-school had been invited, was being planned and all the girls were excited. Whenever the subject was brought up, Rahma blushed and went quiet.

'Do you know anyone at Dillard Court, Rahma?' I enquired. She reddened shyly and Suki guffawed, nudging her.

'Yeah, she does and his name's Kelsey Grey.'

'Shut it, Suki! We danced at last year's party, Cherry, that's all, and he gave me his number. Hey, pack it in, Suki Ito!' laughing at Suki tickling her side.

I squealed. 'Oh, come on, Rahma! Tell me all the goss!'

'There's nothing really to tell. We rarely meet up, if ever. We text one another, natter on Pictapost and Twitter, exchange news by email…'

'…and he sends her flowers for her birthday!' Suki added and Rahma kicked her.

'Plus he already has a girl in his life!'

Rahma said no more. Suki decided to change the subject to her German prep. I was half-listening, my mind on poor Rahma and her attraction to Kelsey Grey. I was lucky to have Danny and pondered on taking our relationship to the next step.

He wrote, 'If a hot guy asks to take you on a date, say no.'

Emboldened by Tasha's disapproval and our argument, and taking advantage of the fact that I was alone in the bathroom, rather than write my response, I spoke it, using the voice messenger: 'We'll see.'

Oh, stuff it, why not take the plunge and invite him for a video chat?

Eighteen
Adam

There was Cherry, no make-up on her beautiful, almost perfect skin and her bewitching large, dazzling blue eyes shining at me. She was in uniform, the top buttons of her blouse open and her tie loose. Consumed by desire, I fought to calm my heart rate down to a normal rhythm.

'I've not got long, prep starts shortly,' she said in that distinctive accent of hers. I recognised a few British dialects from UK TV and hers came from the north of England. There was an attractive earthiness to it. 'Where are you and why do you have your hood up?'

Can't have you seeing the real me, baby.

I'd been surprised to get the video request and was in no position to take it during my Physics tutorial. I decided not to call back yet. When she called again, I happened to be alone in the library, trying to find a book on quantum physics. The librarian had gone home hours ago. I was also wearing my hoodie, another bit of luck. I switched off the main light and kept one of the desk lamps on. I put up my hood and moved into the lamp's shadow. Satisfied I was partially covered on camera, showing my nose and mouth, and checking I was completely alone, I accepted the call.

It was a big moment for both of us and it was no surprise there was an awkward pause as we stared at one another. My blood was pumping and judging by the way she was licking her lips and panting hard, hers was doing the same.

'Hi, baby!'

'Hey,' she said. 'You're in the dark, I can hardly see you.'

'It's the middle of the night,' I lied.

'Where are you?'

'At home.'

'Right. Why is your hood up?'

'I'm a bit shy, baby.'

'*Shy*?' Her laugh tinkled. 'Behave!'

'It's that...' I took a gulp of air, 'often people, erm, what's the word – filter their photos?'

'Do you? Join the club. I do the same if the light isn't right and I have a spot on my chin.' That delightful laugh of hers persecuted me again. She was natural, unfiltered and stunning on screen. 'Please let me see you properly.'

In the background, a ringing sound and a female calling her name stopped her short. *Saved by the bell!*

'Oh, hell, that's Suki. Got to go to prep, soz. I'll try and catch you later, shall I?'

'You do that, baby,' I said.

She blew me a kiss and the screen went off. I sat back in my chair and debated whether there was any way at all to successfully fool her with my fake persona. Petrov was dark and mysterious, I was fair and ordinary. What if I got dark brown contact lenses and had my hair cut and coloured in his style and how would that go down at school? *Fisher fancies Petrov!* Some of the gay lads at school were drawn to him and most suspected Aziz had a serious crush. One afternoon, I overheard a conversation between Carlton-Greene and another lad, Victor Harrington, one of his pals, openly gay and dating a boy in the year above. I was in one of the cubicles, messaging Cherry, my phone on silent, not paying any attention to their discussion until I heard Petrov's name and I gave them my full attention.

'What's on your mind, Harry?' enquired Carlton-Greene, using Harrington's popular nickname.

'I'm really confused, Freddie,' said Harrington.

'Why?'

'I think...' A pause. 'No, I'm *certain* Aziz has the hots for Petrov.'

Carlton-Greene laughed. 'It's taken you long enough to notice and there's you claiming you can spot a gay guy a mile off!'

'I can and I've suspected for ages Aziz batted for the other side. Freddie, I saw him kiss Petrov.'

'*No way!*'

'Straight up, Freddie, a few days ago at rugger practice. The pitch was muddy 'cos of that heavy rain we had the night before.'

'Yeah, that was a horrible day. I had mud in my ears.'

'I'd agreed to stay behind and helped Aziz and Petrov collect the rugby balls. I'd taken the net to the edge of the pitch to pick up a stray and turned round to see Aziz had slipped and pulled Petrov on top of him. Aziz put his arms round him and...'

'*Whoa!* Did anyone else see this?'

'Dunno. I think everyone had gone into the pavilion.'

'How long did it last for?'

'A few seconds.'

'Did Petrov fight him off?'

I drew in my breath, expecting him to say Petrov and Aziz had engaged in an all-out passionate romp. 'He got up pretty sharpish and stormed off, leaving Aziz lying in the mud. I helped Aziz up and he walked away, sniffing, clearly gutted.'

'That'll account for him having a face resembling a smacked arse these past few days,' said Carlton-Greene. I'd also noticed that. 'They've always been tight, though, and seem to be getting pretty well now. Perhaps Aziz misread the signals and said sorry. Petrov can be a contrary bugger, but he will accept an apology. He has a high opinion of Aziz.'

'Aziz refused to confide in me,' said Harrington. 'I think he's embarrassed and in denial. Either way, he won't come out publicly, unless Petrov exposes him.'

'There's no point Petrov doing that,' said Carlton-Greene, chuckling. 'They're mates and I reckon he guessed ages ago Aziz is gay. He's had to learn to be pretty tolerant at The Priory 'cos apparently, homosexuality isn't an accepted thing in Russia.'

I heard the main door open and Harrington rapidly changed the subject.

Eventually, the bathroom emptied of people and it was safe to venture out of the cubicle. I washed my hands and studied my reflection in the mirror, wondering if Petrov and Aziz had made it up in another way. Was it any of my business if they had? Instead, I tried to imagine my life as a Petrov clone. Nope. Bad idea, considering there was no opportunity to dye my hair either at school or at home.

Cherry's attempts to contact me on video were inconvenient at best, whilst I was on the train, for instance, or having dinner at home, not giving me the opportunity to sort out a disguise. I had to give my excuses that I was too busy to talk because Mom and

Dad had my nose to the grindstone; no word of a lie: I had to help them clear out the garage. Dad had brought his old blow torch and other stuff over from the States, intending to sell them in the UK and for some reason not getting round to it. Mom had nagged him into doing it and I'd been roped in to lend a hand.

'If you see anything you fancy, son, by all means take it,' said Dad.

Unlikely, considering it was all junk. Why Dad hadn't already sold this trash in the States was a mystery to me. Mom discussed taking my old toys to the local charity shop and I spotted the blow torch, hidden behind boxes and garden equipment, and dragged it towards me, pressing the switch and the igniter to see if it worked. I jumped in horror at the flash of flame shooting out at me.

'Adam!' Mom ran towards me and Dad held her back.

'Out!' he shouted. The next thing I knew he'd covered my head and I was dragged through the garage door onto the driveway. Outside, Mom freed me and I pulled Dad's jacket from round my head. The torch was lying on the ground and I heard the fire extinguisher going off.

'No harm done,' Dad assured us, his lips twitching.

'His hair's all singed on the top and one side!' wailed Mom.

Shaking, I studied my image in Dad's car wing mirror. 'I look ridiculous!'

Dad properly burst out laughing then. 'I'll give Jacko a call.'

Jacko was the base barber and did one type of cut: a military number one. I always got my hair cut in town where I was guaranteed a proper style.

'Is that necessary?' said Mom, trying to keep her mouth straight.

Within fifteen minutes Jacko arrived carrying his hair clippers. An all-over number one crew cut later, I faced the new me. Mom put antiseptic cream on the burn across my hairline and at that moment I had a bright idea.

Hi, Danny! Nice to meet ya!

Nineteen
Cherry

'What's happened to your hair?'

He was unrecognisable. For a start, he was a lot younger and his eyes were green not the dark brown I'd expected, the reason why I called him my Beautiful Brown-Eyed Baby Boy. He hadn't contradicted me; and surely he wasn't old enough to have an eleven-year-old daughter?

'I got stung by an old blow torch,' he stated, laughing, explaining how his hair had been singed, the burn showing above his hairline and how he'd had to have a number one crew cut. 'What do you think?'

I was truthful. 'Not much. You had lovely hair.'

'It'll grow back. How ya doin', baby?'

'I'm good.' I was happy. 'It's great to see you properly.'

'Disappointed?'

'No, of course I'm not. You're different from your photos, younger, still gorgeous; and – and I love your accent.'

'I love yours, baby. In fact, I love you, period. You're beautiful, my queen.'

I giggled shyly, unsure how anyone could love such a mop-headed fright at six o'clock on a Saturday morning. Giving up on sleep, I'd taken my phone to the kitchen to brew a mug of tea and say 'Hi' to Danny. My hair was all on end and I hadn't had a shower. I ran my fingers through my hair in an effort to give less of the impression I'd been dragged through a hedge backwards. At least I had no spots.

'It's six in the morning here and I'm a mess.'

'You're beautiful. How come you're up this early?'

'I fancied a chat.'

'I have to turn in now, baby. I have work tomorrow. Oh, and there's another call coming through from Christina, to say goodnight.'

'Right,' I said reluctantly, seriously doubting the existence of this daughter. The uncomfortable impression that he was lying refused to go away. We blew kisses to one another and went offline.

Dreamily, I sipped my coffee and gazed out at the dark morning, trying to decide whether I was bothered Danny's appearance on video was different to how he was in his photos. Something was off, but what? I put my coffee mug on the table and sighed. I was no different to many other sixteen-year-old girls: looks mattered. Danny was fit and it had been lovely to meet him on screen. The thing was…

The door to the kitchen opened and Lucy, the domestic who tidied round the school in the mornings every weekend to help top-up her university loan, came in.

'Morning, Cherry,' she said cheerfully. 'You're up early on a Saturday.'

'Yeah; couldn't sleep.' Everyone liked Lucy. She was local to the area and really clever, studying Forensic Science at Cumbria University. 'Do you need a hand clearing up?'

She proceeded to empty the dishwasher. 'No, thanks, I'll have it all done in a jiffy. Why not go for a wander round the grounds? Wrap up warm, mind; it's a bit frosty out there.'

I shivered. 'Nah, it's a bit cold for me. I'm off back to bed. See you later, Lucy.'

'Take care, Cherry.'

Back in the room, Rahma, Suki and Tasha were fast asleep. I climbed back into bed and reached for the book Gran had given to me, a cheesy romance chick lit called *Tainted Roses,* the story of a girl at university chasing her married lecturer. Suki and Rahma were waiting to borrow it. Yawning, my eyes drooped and gradually closed.

I woke up to my phone buzzing. It was another video call from Danny. Why was he calling now? It was stupid o'clock in the morning for him. Suki stirred and moved on her back; the others had no idea I was contacting Danny on video, not daring to risk one of Tasha's snotty lectures. I slipped out of bed, my phone in my dressing-gown pocket, creeping out into the corridor and the privacy of the bathroom four doors away.

'Hi, baby, sorry...' he began.

'What's up?'

'I – I need to speak to you.'

'Why? What's happened?'

'It's my daughter. Christina's very sick.'

'Oh?'

'She has bad pains in her stomach. Mom was calling from the hospital where she took Christina. They think she has appendicitis.'

'Why aren't you there?'

'I'm on my way. You see, baby, we have to pay for our treatment over here. There's no NHS.'

'You have health insurance?'

'Mine's all used up.'

He began to sob.

'Oh, Danny!'

'I ain't got the money for her drugs,' he sniffed.

I frowned. 'It's not right that they'd refuse to treat a kid.'

'That's how it works over here, baby. No money, no treatment. Mom has no insurance left, either.'

'What a stupid system! What are you going to do?'

'If I had the money for the drugs...' he began.

'You work in a bank,' I pointed out. 'Get a loan.'

'I – they fired me.'

'What?'

'I'm sorry. The bank is going through a merger and they've had to cut down on staff...'

'They binned you off,' I finished.

'Excuse me?'

'They got rid of you.'

'Oh. Yes, and now I have no money. I won't get my final wage until the end of the month and I have little saved up. Um, Cherry...'

I waited.

'I was thinking – can you lend me some money?'

Uh? 'What for?'

'For painkillers,' he added. 'Christina needs them.'

'Surely you can get Paracetamol over the counter in America?' I said irritably, the familiar alarm bells ringing in my head.

'Paracetamol ain't strong enough to deaden her pain. Your stepdaddy has money.'

I winced. 'He won't give me any more. I just get my allowance money for school.'

And you're not getting a penny of that.

'Your mom will give you money, won't she? Buy an Amazon voucher and send me the voucher number. It's easy, baby: I can buy painkillers through the Amazon site.'

He was using his daughter's illness to guilt-trip me and it was working! It was wrong and stupid, but I was convinced I was in love enough to give in to him. Ceridwen's messages and comments, including the one I'd deleted that morning, came back to haunt me: *He's a liar, a scammer and he's catfishing you.*

'How – how much do you need?'

Jesus Christ, am I really falling for this?

'Around, say, fifty dollars.'

'Fifty dollars for Paracetamol?'

'No, she needs stronger drugs and they're very expensive.'

I growled. 'We don't have dollars over here, we use pounds. I'm not sure I can buy American vouchers and does Amazon sell medicine?'

'Yes.' He was getting impatient. 'Fifty dollars is somewhere between forty and forty-five of your pounds. All you need to do is buy a voucher from the UK store and send the voucher number to me.'

'How will you use it?'

'My buddy can convert it to a US voucher.'

'Is that legal?'

'No. The thing is, I'm – I'm desperate, my queen. If you loved me, you'd help. *Please*, baby.'

'That's emotional blackmail!'

'I'm sorry, baby. I...'

'I'll do it.'

'Really?'

'I'll borrow off my mum.' No way was I going to use my own money. I had this peculiar notion that if I sponged off Mum it'd be less of a problem. 'I'll buy the Amazon voucher and...'

'Please hurry.'

'I'll let you know.'

You stupid cow, Cherry, giving in to him!

Except if it was true and the kid had appendicitis and needed painkillers he'd hate me if I didn't help.

'I understand. Thank you, baby! I love you!'

'Right; and what if she needs an operation?'

'Leave me to sort it. It's not certain she needs the op. I'll work it out somehow. You've done more than enough.'

I certainly have!

'Will you tell me what happens to Christina?' I choked.

'Of course I will, my queen. Thank you for caring. I…'

I abruptly ended the call and he sent a love emoji. To punish him, I purposely delayed getting back to him for half an hour, adding a couple of meaningless kisses and went offline.

Later, I rang Mum.

'What do you need the money for?' she queried suspiciously.

'For – a new hockey stick.'

'Why? What happened to yours?'

'It broke in half in the last match.'

'I can buy you one in the holidays. Isn't there a spare you can use?'

'No.'

A long pause followed.

'What if I order one online and have it sent to the school?'

'Mum, I...'

'Cherry!' Mum's tone suddenly changed. She'd always been such a gentle person, not really a soft touch; since marrying Greg, though, she'd become harder somehow. 'Be honest, Cherry Hill, what do you really need forty quid for? Do you owe money? Have you been gambling?'

'Mum! No, I haven't!'

'Are you drinking, taking drugs?'

'Seriously, Mum!' I bit my nail. 'It's for – a mate.'

'At Helton? They're all minted.'

'No. It's for Precious.'

'Why?'

Think fast, Cherry!

'To buy her a nice present for her sixteenth birthday; it's this month.' That bit at least was true. 'I really miss her and Suze.'

Liar!

Mum grunted down the phone. 'It's a lot of money to spend and Precious will think you're showing off and flashing the cash. Haven't you got enough in your savings to buy her a present? Greg gives you a good allowance.'

'Yeah, I have,' I murmured.

'Are you OK, Cherry?' Mum was suddenly on alert. 'You're not being bullied, are you? I thought you'd settled down at Helton; you said you had new friends. What's really going on, love? You can tell your old mum. I won't judge, I promise.'

You will. There's no way you'll understand.

'It doesn't matter. Forget it,' I said snappily and changed the subject back to Christmas.

'We're going to Spain for New Year now,' she said.

'How come?'

'I told him no way was I spending Christmas without you. If he's that keen to go, he can go on his own.'

'How did he take it?'

'He's lumping it.'

I laughed, happy she'd stood up for both of us.

Our conversation over, I stewed over Danny's request for money in frustration. Forty pounds was a lot of money to give to a person I'd never met and I resented dipping into my savings. A message came through at the end of last lesson: 'Are you there, baby? Do you have the Amazon voucher now?'

I swore silently. Thanks to the heavy snow, shopping parties to town had been cancelled, meaning I couldn't go to Tesco to buy one. There was always an e-voucher, I suppose…

Leaving the bedroom, I bumped into Suki coming out of the bathroom opposite and said, 'Got any rum left in your drawer?'

Let Danny wait.

'Yeah, fill your boots.' She grasped my hand. 'Darling, you're really pale. Tell Auntie Suki what's wrong.'

Three shots later and a refusal to submit to any further questioning, she took the bottle off me and tucked me up in bed.

Twenty
Adam

It was obscene how I had Cherry right where I wanted her. I was a nice guy and hadn't acted this crazy ever, yet I had to stay focused on my revenge. Cherry had hurt me by blocking the real me, Adam, and I hadn't got over what had happened in Helton. I blamed Petrov for all of it, of course; by tagging that snap of Cherry he'd begun a chain of events there was no going back from. I was in deep and had crossed the line. They say you always hurt the one you love, although I was more certain of it merely being lust these days.

This is really about Petrov and Cherry being collateral damage, isn't it?

Why was I asking her for money? Was it that I was twisted, enjoying goading her and to paint Petrov/Danny blacker than he already was? I was making it up as I went along. I expected some resistance over the Amazon voucher and it was no surprise I ended up having to plead for it. She sent through the code and a sadistic sort of thrill took hold of me I tried to push to one side. Of course, Cherry had no inkling I was in England and cashing the voucher was no problem because I had a UK Amazon account and was able to spend the vouchers easily.

'How will you spend it?' she asked.

'I told you, my pal knows how to convert the British vouchers to American.'

'How?'

'It's kind of – secret.'

'Dodgy?'

'I guess.'

'I hope you get the meds your daughter needs.'

'Thanks.'

'Is she having the operation?'

'They think she has gastroenteritis now, not appendicitis,' I said, amazed at how easy it was to lie. 'They're sending her home later. She's dehydrated and has to drink plenty of water.'

'That's good. Not much of a hospital bill. What's the medication for?'

'To stop her vomiting and diarrhoea and kill the bug in her insides.'

'Oh, right. I hope everything turns out.'

'Thanks, baby.'

I sent her a love heart and hoped she'd bought what I'd told her. A message pinged from that troll Ceridwen: 'Catfishing thief!' I was unsettled by the shame of deceiving Cherry, and fretting that somehow Ceridwen knew what I'd been up to. I deleted the message and blocked her again.

It was easy pickings, small amounts, ten dollars here, twenty dollars there, making up various reasons why I needed the money. There were always questions: why not borrow off my mom and get another job?

'If you love me, baby, you'll help me,' I said. She always gave in and the vouchers came, Amazon, iTunes, and always self-reproach nudged at my conscience.

Spending the money on me and my family was wrong somehow and Mom was bound to enquire why I was buying her gifts all of a sudden. Maybe I'd use it on Petrov, a kind of compensation for stealing his identity. His sixteenth birthday was on the last but one day of the semester and the class had planned a get-together at midnight to make it a double celebration. There were no classes on the last day and it was hoped the authorities might turn a blind eye if they heard any illegal partying. Hangovers were anticipated due to the quantity of liquor to be consumed. Everyone in the class was expected to contribute a small gift for Petrov and food for the celebrations. I got a big cake from the local store. The alcohol was to be bought separately by five of the boys out of town and smuggled in somehow. The hoard was stuffed at the back of closets and in lockers. One thing I hadn't done was to buy Petrov a gift, unwilling to spend my own money on that.

***

Safely in the dorm, away from the rest of the school partying downstairs with girls invited from local schools, I started a video to Cherry, the faint bass of party music in the background.

'Christina's good, I think.'

I'd practised the downcast, disappointed tone over and over again I was expert at it. I'd brought some clippers to school and shaved my head again to maintain my new look. My haircut had caused a sensation among my classmates.

'Bit drastic,' Carlton-Greene had remarked. 'Where did the burn come from?'

I related the sorry tale of the blow torch and the military barber and he laughed. 'Oh, I see. It suits you.'

Now Cherry was saying, 'What d'you mean, you think?'

'I haven't seen her lately,' I told her. 'She's not speaking to me. Her birthday's coming up and she's after a pair of Wi-Fi headphones, the trouble is they cost seventy-five dollars and I explained I don't have that kind of money right now. It sucks not being able to buy her things.'

'She sounds a right spoilt brat,' Cherry commented. 'I had to save up for stuff at her age.'

'You're rich now, right?'

I sensed a flicker of annoyance.

'Sorry, Danny, no; I won't do it.'

'No to what? What did I say?'

'I'm not sending you any more Amazon vouchers.' She was getting angry.

'The cheapest headphones are on Amazon. I'll pay you back. Please, baby! I miss my little girl!'

'Oh, sod off, Danny!'

Off went the video. 'Shit!' I'd overdone it and that was confirmed less than five minutes later.

'I've had enough,' she wrote. 'I'm not your personal bank account. Get another job and tell the lazy little cow to save up for the headphones. I've had enough of you pestering me for money. See yer.'

And I was blocked.

Throwing my phone on the bed in frustration, I was startled by Petrov coming in and saying, 'What are you doing in here? You're missing all the fun.'

He was carrying two open bottles of Pepsi cola in one hand and a slice of the birthday cake I'd bought in the other. Flustered by his unexpected arrival and exasperated at the interruption, I lied, 'I had to call my mom.'

'Here you go,' he said, handing over one of the bottles.

'Thanks.' I took a sip, more than a bit disturbed at how much nicer he'd been to me lately. 'What else can I taste?' I detected a distinct hint of spirit. 'And you've cut the cake already.'

'There's a shot of rum in it,' Petrov laughed, 'courtesy of Freddie. He sneaked it in. I get the impression you need it; that was a pretty heavy conversation you were having. I'm told the cake's delicious, by the way. There's plenty left over for everyone. Thank you for buying it.'

'Oh, it was nothing, really. Sorry for not getting you a gift.' This was the longest conversation we'd ever had. The rum was lowering my inhibitions and I was happy he liked the cake. 'Mom was winding me up, is all.' I didn't go into detail, not being able to think up a story. 'Are you allowed to drink and eat cake if you have diabetes?'

'I can have one drink and that's my limit. I'm not a great drinker and I haven't touched the cake. Let's call that my gift.'

Flustered by these unexpected pleasantries, I was trembling inside.

'How – how did you know I was here?' I stammered.

'I saw you leave.'

I was embarrassingly conscious of the heat rising in my body. *Will you please quit staring and licking your lips!*

'I came to bring you back to the party. You were missed.'

'Was I?'

'Yes.'

Who by?

'And you decided to check out the dormitory,' I finished, putting my hands together on the bottle to keep them steady.

I was rapidly melting under his spell. He reached for my bottle and took it from me, placing it on my bedside locker and putting his down beside it. Soon I was in his arms and he was raining kisses on my lips, fast ensnaring me in his web. All kinds of wrong! The image of Cherry I was trying to force in my mind, her image, her body, vanished in his embrace.

Consumed by disgust, I scrambled out of bed and grabbed my bath towel from its rail to wrap round my waist, keeping my back to him, my chest heaving, afraid I was going to puke and pass out.

'Admit it, my love,' whispered Petrov, 'this has been coming for months.'

My whole body was quaking. 'Not for me, it hasn't, and I'm not your love!'

'There's no denying the chemistry between us.'

'I'm not gay or even bi! There's a girl...!'

'She's not here and I am.'

Refusing to hear any more, I grabbed the gel from my locker and headed for the showers, locking the door, half-expecting him to knock and request to join me. The shower water, and my tears, flowed over me. I put my hand against the tiles and threw up, miserably watching the bile vanish slowly down the drain.

What have I done!

The shower gel did nothing to wash away the memory of the last half-hour, the smell and feel of him remained. I burst into fresh sobbing and sank down on the floor. It mustn't happen again. I'd been frustrated I couldn't have Cherry, was all; I'd used him, made him happy and we'd both got what we needed out of it.

And Cherry hadn't crossed my mind once.

Happy birthday, Petrov!

I dug my nails into my palms, incapable of understanding what had happened. During the whole process, being caught in action hadn't been on our minds. I was apprehensive of Dad's fury if my parents got to hear of it and puked again. What if Petrov blabbed? What if he boasted to the others? Had he done it for a bet? Panicking, and needing answers to those questions, I got to my feet, turned off the shower, grabbed the towel and wrapped it round my body, returning nervously to the dormitory. Petrov had gone and there were clean sheets on my bed (where were the old ones?) my clothes neatly folded on the pillow. My phone buzzed in my jeans pocket and the text read, '♥ xxx'.

Somehow I managed to get through the rest of that evening, in spite of a desire to pack my case and beat it out of there; the problem was I had nowhere to go apart from home and the inevitable interrogations from Mom and Dad. I was no longer safe in Petrov's company; my yearning for him was too strong to trust myself around him and no matter what, I had to persuade Mom to let me leave The Priory and not go back next semester. I concocted all sorts of incredible excuses, one being that Petrov had assaulted me, except what was the point in telling such a lie and needlessly ruining his life? Throwing my guts up was therapeutic and gave me the strength to calm down. I swallowed a couple of painkillers, got dressed and went to the hall, fearful of the reaction to my late arrival, which, mercifully, turned out to be a non-event.

Mingling and behaving as if I hadn't a care in the world was an enormous challenge. I was really thirsty and drank water, cola and lemonade, refusing Carlton-Greene's offer of liquor that was hidden under the tables, to spice up my glass. I had to stay sober. Getting drunk, angry, causing a scene and calling out Petrov meant a third strike and subsequent exclusion.

I surveyed my schoolmates and their pretty dancing partners, and sensing Petrov's presence, we were briefly locked together in a moment of passionate longing. He was standing next to a beautiful Asian girl wearing a sari, not listening to what she was saying. His whole, seductive attention was on me. My breathing got faster and in an attempt to get out of his way, I went up to the nearest girl and invited her to dance.

The party broke up at eleven-thirty. The Sixth Form helped to clear up and the rest of the school was packed off to bed. Of course, Year Eleven was buzzing because of Petrov's party at midnight, something I'd completely forgotten under the circumstances. Why had that idiot Carlton-Greene offered to host it in our dorm? I needn't have worried: Petrov appeared to read my mind, perhaps trying to spare my discomfort by joining a group at the far end of the room, remaining sober on bottled water, and observing everyone else getting drunker on illicit booze. Unfortunately, I misinterpreted his actions to be a snub and, growing more and more infuriated, I sat alone, glaring at him. He continued to ignore me and was monopolised almost exclusively by Aziz. My non-drinking policy waned in my despondency and I reached for a bottle of gin, becoming drunker and louder, fuelling arguments over soccer and rugby, to the point where I was getting more erratic by the minute and many a glass got smashed in the process.

'Come on, Fisher, you're overdoing it,' warned Carlton-Greene, taking my glass away. 'You'd better lie down before a teacher walks in to investigate the noise.'

He guided me to my bed, where earlier I'd enjoyed my humiliation.

A bed now seriously tainted by sin.

I laughed and pulled Carlton-Greene on top of me.

'Kiss me, Freddie!'

Snorting, Carlton-Greene calmly removed my arms from around his neck.

'Help me, fellas! He's wasted. And fetch a bowl from the bathroom. I can see all that booze coming right back up.'

My clothes were removed and, ashamed for fantasising it was Petrov who'd undressed me, I was put into my pyjamas. The last person I needed near me right now, he grabbed a chair and sat down next to me.

'Poor Adam, I was hoping to see you happy tonight,' he said sadly. 'Instead you are very sad and I cannot bear that. What can I do to help you? I…'

'The best thing you can do,' I snarled at him, 'is to piss off and leave me alone.'

I turned my back on him, not caring if I hurt his feelings.

'Sweet dreams,' he purred.

I heard Aziz saying, 'Come on, birthday boy, he'll live. You're missing your party and haven't opened any of your presents yet.'

'Coming.'

My back to the room, feigning sleep and attempting to hide all traces of my misery, I imagined Petrov's arm around Aziz and succumbed to an overwhelming sense of jealousy, imagining them getting closer and closer.

At nearly three in the morning, the party broke up and people drifted away to their beds. I failed to sleep, my brain hounded by images of Petrov, and only Petrov.

Twenty-One
Cherry

It was no good. No matter how hard I tried to forget Danny, I was struggling to get through life without him. It had been two days since I'd blocked him and I was drowning in desolation, pining all day and crying myself to sleep at night, despite my anger at how he was always nagging me for money. Why did he do that? It was almost twisted. Whenever I gave in to him and sent photos, my head questioned: *what was I getting in return?*

Someone to love, my heart replied, *and how sad is that?*

I was beginning to think Ceridwen was right: Danny *was* a catfish and I'd refused to acknowledge it. Even so, denial continued to linger. Hearing the other girls discussing boys back home fuelled my yearning for him. I went round hiding my state of despair, imagining my world without him. The evening we were getting ready for the Christmas party I unblocked him and sent him a love emoji.

I imagined Ceridwen echoing the words I found hard to push away: *what did you do that for?*

And I was unable to make sense of any of it.

Suki, holding up two of her beautiful party dresses on their hangers and trying to decide the best one to wear for the Christmas party, saw me on my phone and said, 'Leave Danny alone now, Cherry.' I hadn't told her I'd blocked him and Rahma had commented that morning she'd not heard me say his name for three days. 'Give me your opinion: the coral or the blue?'

I admired them both, Harrods-bought and very expensive. The straight, lacy coral had a square neckline, and the velvet blue a strapped bodice, tucked-in waist, a black thin sequined belt and a flowing skirt. Both were very short in length; Suki loved to show off her long, slim legs to their full extent and in either dress she'd be a knockout.

'The blue,' I said.

'The coral is more fetching,' said Rahma, already in her outfit, a gorgeous three piece of a chiffon black bolero over a green silk, strapped blouse and skirt that showed off her hourglass figure, and high-heeled, strapped shoes displaying diamante buckles. Her hair was immaculate in long braids and colourful beads and she was putting the finishing touches to her make-up. Kelsey Grey would be blown away.

'The blue it is, darlings!' said Suki and Rahma stuck her tongue out. Tasha was also undecided between going casual in jeans and T-shirt and wearing a stunning dress she'd been given by her sister for her birthday, a long, pale aqua V-neck gown.

'Not jeans, Tash!' Suki threw her dresses on her bed, grabbed Tasha's jeans from her and chucked them in her wardrobe. 'No way! You're wearing the dress!'

'I'm more comfortable in jeans,' Tasha protested. 'You know how I hate dressing up.'

'It's a lovely dress and you must repay your sister's generosity by wearing it. Now put it on and we'll do your hair and make-up and send her a photo. Cherry?'

I jumped. 'What?'

Danny had sent two shocked emojis and written, 'Baby! This is a lovely surprise! You said you weren't speaking to me any more!'

Suki throwing a bath towel prevented me from typing back. 'You haven't had a shower. Hurry up, you'll be late.'

Tutting, I put my phone in my dressing-gown pocket and dug out my shower gel. Like Tasha, I preferred to go casual, having nothing in my wardrobe compared to the other girls. Suki and Rahma had dragged me out to Kendal the previous weekend, wearing me out by forcing me to try on all the outfits and shoes. Finally, they decided – not me! – on a sparkling, dark purple, off-the-shoulder skater dress and black calf-length boots.

'Stunning!' remarked Rahma. Examining my reflection in the long mirror, I had to agree.

'You need a necklace,' said Tasha, now beautiful in her dress, her hair loose and her make-up flawless. 'I have some purple glass beads that will do nicely.'

The beads were great, jagged and oval-shaped, and suited the dress perfectly. I took a selfie and sent it to Danny.

'Amazing,' he wrote back. 'I love you, my queen.'

My stomach flipped over. I was happy again. All that had gone on previously was forgotten, apart from the warnings in my head: *say no if he hassles you for more money* and I was determined to listen.

Another message came from Danny as we wandered to the Assembly Hall where the Christmas dance was being held: 'You're good enough to eat! Promise me you won't fall head over heels for one of those lads at the dance.'

I promised, having no intention of falling for a schoolboy tonight; I was in love with a real man.

Everyone was dressed up to the nines, the girls and female teachers in their colourful gowns and outfits, the male teachers and the boys from Dillard Court School dressed in smart suits, trousers and shirts of all styles and colours. Food and drink covered every inch of the tables, banners and balloons hung on the ceiling and the walls, and we mingled. Rahma was searching the people in the room eagerly.

'Kelsey Grey,' Suki hissed to me.

A very attractive lad of around seventeen had tapped Rahma on the shoulder. 'Looking for me?'

'Kelsey!' Rahma grinned broadly. 'Hi!'

'Hello, beautiful,' he said, putting his arm around her waist. Rahma giggled and hugged him.

'Kelsey, you remember Suki and Tasha, and this is Cherry. She's new this term.'

It was easy to see why Rahma fancied Kelsey. He had big blue eyes and flawless, tanned skin. Suki had told me he was from a titled family, the fourth son of a duke.

'Nice to meet you, Cherry,' he said. 'May I say how ravishing you ladies look tonight?'

'You're full of it, Kelsey,' said Suki good-naturedly.

Kelsey blew a kiss at her and swept a euphoric Rahma off to dance. The DJ was playing the number one single in the charts.

'It's great to see Rahma happy,' said Suki, beaming at Kelsey taking Rahma in his arms for their first dance. 'She deserves to be. She's really into Kelsey and he's very sweet and charming, but I wonder if he's trying to have his cake and eat it.'

'Rahma knows the other girl exists,' Tasha pointed out, pouring lemonade into her glass. 'She won't let Kelsey take advantage, she's not that naive. It's a bit of fun for her and can't go anywhere, whether he's the son of a duke or not. Her dad won't let her marry a Brit.'

'Who's the other girl?' I asked.

'Oh, some bit of skirt from an upper class family in the town where Kelsey lives,' said Suki in the down-to-earth way she often used that always amused me, in view of her own privileged background. 'The Honourable Lady Snooty Knickers from Some Posh Family, nothing compared to Rahma. My objection is Kelsey's still seeing her and knocking her up, probably. I've warned Rahma to be careful.'

'Rahma's got her head screwed on,' I said comfortingly. 'If they don't see each other that often surely there isn't anything more to it than them being friends.'

'The thing is, Cherry, Rahma wishes it was more than that. If that other girl was out of the way, she'd be prepared to see Kelsey behind her dad's back.'

While understanding Suki's reservations, Rahma was blissfully happy in Kelsey's arms now and that was all that mattered.

'Poor Rahma,' said Tasha, nodding appreciatively at a lad approaching her to claim a dance. 'Her dad's such a dick.'

Shortly, we were all dancing. Suki was spoilt for choice, surrounded by lads, all vying for her attention. Tasha was monopolised by one in particular, the handsome Jack Shakespeare, apparently a distant descendant of William Shakespeare. It was lovely to see her enjoying herself.

'I bet you're glad you dressed up now,' I said to her, selecting some food from the buffet. Rahma was glued to Kelsey and Suki was surrounded by a group of lads. 'You're a knockout in that dress! I'm not surprised Jack's paying you a lot of attention.'

Jack had joined some of his mates and kept looking over at a blushing Tasha.

'Yeah, he's nice,' she said shyly.

'Suki's very popular,' I remarked, laughing. Boys kept bringing her food and drinks. She relished playing the field all over Helton and back home in Japan.

'She always is,' said Tasha, chuckling. 'How are you enjoying the party, Cherry?

I sipped my lemonade. 'Yeah, it's great fun.'

'Keen on any of the boys you've met so far?'

'No one in particular stands out.'

'Not even him?'

She gestured at a dark-haired lad sitting on the edge of the stage, talking to a couple of his mates standing below him. At intervals, he glanced across at me and I was transfixed, managing to stare him out for a moment until I decided it was disconcerting and he was winning the battle. Dazed and flushed, I turned back to Tasha quickly. I reached for a sandwich, trying to resist being drawn into his gaze again.

'Cherry?' Tasha was saying.

'Sorry, what?'

'Him.' She pointed directly at the lad and I shrugged, trying to act casual.

'Oh. I haven't danced…'

'He hasn't taken his eyes off you all evening.'

Not wrong there; they were boring into me, causing my skin to tingle.

'It's true,' went on Tasha. 'One of his mates said...'

'Tasha!'

'He did!' Tasha was clearly enjoying my embarrassment. 'That's Lord Robert Davison-Hall and he's Sports Captain at Dillard. I can tell from here he fancies you.'

My knees were knocking. 'You mean he fancies himself! Will his face crack if he smiles?'

'If you smile at him he might smile back.'

By now, my cheeks were burning. 'Get lost, Tash!'

'Go on, I dare you. What harm can it do?'

'Haha, Tash, you're wicked!'

She refused to let up, so I humoured her. He frowned at me for a few more seconds and turned away, leaving me surprised by how disappointed I was.

'There you go,' I said irritably, turning my attention to the food on the table. 'He's a weirdo...'

Tasha nudged me urgently. 'Cherry!' she hissed. 'He's coming over!'

Without a word, he put his hand on my arm. Spellbound, and the blood rushing in my ears, I forgot Tasha and everyone in the room and let him drag me away. Glancing back, I noticed Jack had appeared at Tasha's side and she'd lost interest in me.

I collapsed on my bed, frightened and ashamed. I'd enjoyed it and hadn't wanted it to stop.

If anyone had noticed us going through the door that led to the staircase behind the stage, there'd been no attempt to find out where we were going. I was terrified by the way he was pulling me along, his silence unsettling. Thinking back, I'd been stupid not to shout for help.

'Slow down, will you?' I gasped, trying to wriggle my wrist free of his tight grasp. 'Hey, are you deaf? I said...'

He cut me short. 'Will the dressing-rooms be open?'

'No idea, I've never been backstage. Hey!' I lifted my hand and bit his wrist. 'I said let go of me!

I expected him to smack me in the mouth for doing that and was fully prepared to hit him back. Even though he was physically stronger, I was good at scratching, kicking and biting. Acting excited and turned on, he gawped at my heaving chest and said, 'Let's try one of the doors, shall we?'

He grabbed the top of my arm and pulled me over to the nearest door opening to a store cupboard containing props and costumes hanging on rails. He turned on the light and closed the door behind us.

'I'm getting out of here,' I declared, and brought my knee up to his groin, causing him to double-up in pain, and saw my chance to escape. Reaching forward, he grabbed me round the waist and wrestled me to the floor, putting his hand over my mouth to silence my screams and pinning my arms back to prevent me from punching at him.

'You'll hurt yourself if you keep struggling,' he said.

'That's a funny thing to say to somebody you're going to rape!' I growled angrily, trying to fight him off.

I moaned pleasurably at the feel of his lips on my neck and my resistance melted in his embrace.

'I won't do that,' he said softly. 'You're beautiful. Your name's Cherry, right? I'm Robert. It's nice to meet you, Cherryhillpie – no, I beg your pardon, Queencherrybaby.'

My heart pumped hard against him. 'You've seen me on Pictapost?'

'I'm one of your many admirers, yes. Lord Bob at your service.'

I didn't get the chance to tell him I had no memory of a Lord Bob.

'Cherry! Wait!'

I ignored his appeals to stay, ran out of the room and ducked into the nearest toilet cubicle, locked the door, fastened my bra, pulled on my dress and grimaced at my untidy hair and smudged lipstick in the mirror. I couldn't go back to the party looking like a tramp. I ran my fingers through my ruffled hair and used toilet paper to wipe off the smeared lippy.

Puffing out my cheeks, I left the cubicle and went back to the party. Thankfully, there was no sign of Lord Robert and I went back out into the hall, trying not to seem conspicuous.

'Cherry?' Tasha was anxious. 'I've been looking everywhere for you. What's up? You're pale. Are you ill? Shall I get Matron?'

'No,' I said abruptly. 'I'm good, thanks, Tash,' and left for Rowan House and Room Five, where I collapsed on my bed and sobbed.

Following the break-up of the party, Tasha, Suki and Rahma came bouncing in and I was in bed, feigning sleep, putting my head under my pillow to try and drown them out.

Shut up!

Miss Carter came to my rescue. 'Into bed now, you lot. It's late and you have classes tomorrow.'

Thank you! Peace at last!

A couple of days later, a bouquet of beautiful yellow roses arrived for me and the card read: *Thank you for a wonderful evening. R xxx.*

'Oh, yeah?' Suki nudged me and everyone else crowded round oohing and aahing. 'Who's the lucky fella, eh, Cherry, you dark horse!'

Tasha jumped in, 'She met him last night!' and chuckled slyly, saying no more. I sniffed the roses to hide my delight and kept my mouth firmly shut.

Twenty-Two
Adam

The memory of my encounter with Petrov haunted me throughout the Christmas vacation, not helped by his text on the last day of the semester sending me compliments of the season, returned by me out of politeness. All too swiftly, the holiday drew to a close and the new term got closer. I became more and more uneasy, trying to battle on and contacting Cherry frequently, telling her how much I loved her. Who the hell was I fooling, me or her? Kissing my favourite photo of her was no help eliminating the reality of what had happened and I was forced to reassess my sexuality: was I straight, gay, bi? Was it possible to be exclusively heterosexual if I relished the touch of another person of the same gender? I had no one to confide in, especially not my parents. Self-recrimination plagued my soul and I was frantic to recapture my attraction to Cherry. Photos and videos weren't enough: I had to see her in the flesh, meet up, and prove I wasn't gay; Cherry was the closest thing I had to a normal boy/girl relationship. In an attempt to win her trust again, I steered clear of the subject of money and begged for more revealing photos, cleavage and skimpy panty shots. Lusting over them calmed the doubts over my sexuality.

As it turned out, I lost the chance to tell Mom and Dad that I'd had enough of The Priory. On Boxing Day, Mom collapsed, was rushed to hospital and taken into surgery.

The doctor came to give us an update. She'd had what was called an ectopic pregnancy, which he explained was a baby growing in a woman's ovarian tube and it had to come out. The operation had been a success and she'd recover physically; obviously, it was expected she'd take longer to get over it psychologically. Sadly, she'd lost the tube and probably the chance of ever having another baby. Dad sat down and placed his head in his hands.

Stunned, I said, 'Sorry, Dad. I had no idea you and Mom were trying for another kid.'

Tear-stained, he hugged me to him.

'It's been on our radar for a while, champ. We love the hell out of you and always hoped for another Adam or Eve to be proud of.'

That made up my mind not to let Mom down by announcing my intention to leave school. Not the right moment again. She was really frail and sobbed, 'I'm sorry.'

'It's OK, honey,' said Dad, tears in his eyes, his hand on hers. 'You're going to be fine, that's all that matters, and the doctor said it's not altogether hopeless.'

I lay down on the bed beside her and she kissed me and held me close. If only I could rewind my life back to being a little kid in the States, protected and loved, rather than being considered old enough to take responsibility for my own decisions and lead an independent life. Getting the story of what had passed between me and Petrov off my chest was a pipedream. On the day Mom had got sick, I'd played the scene over in my head, sitting them down and saying, 'Mom, Dad, listen...'

Dad shook me awake. 'Come on, son, visiting's over. We have to go and let your mom get some rest.'

I wiped my eyes. The clock on the wall said it had gone nine in the evening. The nurse came to shoo us out. We'd been there most of the day and were ready for our beds. Infuriatingly, sleep eluded me and not only because of my worry for Mom. My sense of disgrace mounted to the surface again and without success I willed my worship for Petrov to go away. I swore at a message from another Ceridwen account and deleted it angrily.

Later at home, from Cherry came, 'Where are you? I've been calling and calling and you haven't called or messaged me back.'

I growled, my mood worsening by the second. 'Sorry, baby. I've been at the hospital. My mom was taken ill.'

'Really.' Not a question, more of a, 'Oh, is that right' comment.

Christ, my mom is sick and all this selfish bitch can do is gripe!

'Yeah. She had to have an urgent op. Women's stuff.' I added a sad emoji for good measure.

Another lie incoming: if I told Cherry I was taking care of my fictitious daughter, she'd probably request to meet her on video.

'Christina's gone to my aunt's, Mom's sister. She lives in the same town.'

'Oh.'

'I live further away and have no job.' I had to put an end to this dangerous, aggravating inquisition. 'Why do you always question everything I tell you, baby?'

'You're playing me. You keep saying you'll visit and always find excuses not to.'

'I ain't got the cash to fly to the UK, my queen.'

Another pause. 'What if I sent you the money?'

Totally unexpected!

'Danny, will you come if I send you the money for the flight? We can get a room in a small hotel. I love you, my Beautiful Brown-Eyed Baby Boy!'

WOW, an open invitation! Handing it to me on a plate!

Wait, I had to be careful. After the events in Helton, what if it was a trap? There was also the fact I looked nothing like Petrov and she'd figure that, at just turned sixteen, no way was I old enough to be anyone's dad. My spine tingled in anticipation of using plenty of coercion to win her round. Surely that meant I was straight or at least bi?

No, not bi, not ever!

A few minutes sensible, reasonable, soul-searching passed and I said, 'No, my darling. My mom's sick.'

'Right,' she said, 'I'll come to you.'

Uh?

'No, my love,' I wrote hastily.

'Why not?'

Shit, what do I tell her?

'You're not really in America, are you?'

Ceridwen again! Great bloody timing! Immediately, Cherry began a video and forgetting it was supposed to be around ten-thirty in the morning in America, I joined her.

Cherry was incredulous. 'Did you see *that*?'

'She sent it to both of us. Has she hacked into our conversation somehow?'

'Surely it's not possible for her to do that?'

'You're right saying she's a witch,' I said bitterly, relieved Cherry hadn't taken any notice of what she'd written.

She changed the subject. 'How come you're in the dark? Isn't it morning where you are?'

I always had to think fast during these irritating encounters and I suddenly sounded listless and pathetic. 'The curtains are closed. I have a terrible migraine 'cos I was at the hospital visiting Mom and barely slept all night.'

'Oh. I'm sorry you get migraines and your mum's poorly,' she said, her concern genuine.

'Yeah and my diabetes adds to the problem.' It was frightening how easy it was to lie and of course my inspiration was Petrov, using his photos to catfish this girl, the guy I was trying to convince myself I had no feelings for. 'Every so often I get these awful headaches and I have to lie down in my room in the dark.'

'Doesn't your phone screen irritate you?'

'Sure, it's the flickering that does it.'

'I'll go, let you rest,' she said disappointedly.

'Good idea,' I said, failing to be shocked by my lies, my tiredness and upset over Mom overtaking my reason.

'Danny,' she said hesitantly, 'do you fancy me?'

'I – of course I do, baby.'

'If you won't come to me, why shouldn't I come to you?'

'It's a long way and...'

'Ceridwen said she thinks you're not in America.' Her tone was suspicious, accusing.

'Take no notice of her,' I said. 'She's a shit-stirrer.'

'What about the money?'

'I haven't asked for money today.'

'And tomorrow?'

'No, I promise. I'll go elsewhere in future.' I gave the deliberate impression I was hurt and she bit her lip.

'I'm sorry, Danny.'

'Forget it. If you believe I'm a scammer and catfish that's your problem. I came to you for help because I trusted you and thought you loved me. I'd be there for you.'

'Oh, Danny!' Cherry's beautiful eyes were filling up. 'I *do* love you!'

'So you say!'

'I do! I'm sorry!'

'Good.' I was losing respect for this easy target. She was trusting, gullible and ready to accept any old shit I fed her. 'I'll message you tomorrow, right? I have to go now. My head is aching and I need to rest.'

I went offline and climbed into bed. Shortly, a message and a photo came through. Taking in the milky white skin and the right full breast almost fully exposed by the deliberately fallen bra strap aroused a deep-rooted desire within me. There was no doubt Cherry was gorgeous, but I was overwhelmed by my need for Petrov.

I'm sorry, Cherry; it's Petrov I love, not you!

It was true. Denial was useless.

Imagine Scott and Dean's faces if I told them that!

I kissed Cherry's photo and another notification came through from that Ceridwen: 'Tell her the truth.'

My blood boiled. I'd had enough of this idiot. Rather than deleting the message, I accepted it. 'Fuck off and quit trolling me and my girl!'

Almost immediately the message was read.

'I'm your worst nightmare and she's not your girl. You're catfishing her.'

'Where's your proof I'm a catfish? You don't know me!'

'I know more than you think. You're using photos from another account and pretending to be someone you're not.'

Deciding I had to see this Ceridwen in person, I opened the video and immediately she went offline.

Was she guessing? She was certain I was up to no good and it was troubling. Muttering, I reported the account for harassment again.

Meanwhile, I was desperate to prove I was straight and Cherry was offering her body and soul to me, but I was nervous: what if Cherry told that girl what she was planning and she tried to attack me again? It occurred to me that she was jealous Cherry had an online boyfriend: what if *she* had a thing for Cherry, the way Petrov had one for me?

In the dorm, I sent Cherry a message: 'Your roommates know I exist, right?'

Five minutes later: 'Yeah, they do.'

'Have you told them we're hooking up?'

'No. One of them – well, she won't be happy.'

'Why not?'

'She's the one whose best mate committed suicide over that boy she met on Pictapost.' *My attacker, maybe?* 'You'll come?'

'Yes, if it remains our secret,' I said hesitantly. 'I'd hate it if anyone hassled you into changing your mind. I'll get the dough.' Half a dozen love emojis sent. 'Send me the details of where we're to meet. Love you.'

I logged off and attempted sleep, my dreams tormented again by Petrov.

Twenty-Three
Cherry

It was all arranged. We were going to meet up during the holidays, not in a hotel, at Gran and Granddad's bungalow: they were off to visit Gran's sister in Ireland at New Year for a week and Gran had requested I house sit if Mum agreed, meaning I'd get away from slimy Greg and Jeremy and have a wonderful few days with Danny. Perfect! Of course, Mum took some persuading until, in the end, Gran swayed her.

'She's sixteen, love, and a sensible girl,' Gran had said. I bit into a biscuit and suppressed a smirk. *If only she knew!* 'It's not fair leaving her to rattle around on her own in that massive house and she can have her mates here, that way His Nibs can't complain if his valuables go missing.' Mum scowled. Gran always called Greg 'His Nibs'. 'Cara from next door said she'd pop round every day to check up on her.'

I rolled my eyes. Cara Frederic was Gran's mate and also the street busybody.

'You win,' Mum had conceded. 'I hear what you're saying. Leaving her alone at the Hall won't be much fun for her and Tulip's going home for the holidays. No parties, Cherry, d'you hear me?'

'Yes, Mum.'

'You're welcome to have your mates round for company, love,' added Gran.

'Cheers, Gran.'

Not happening. There'd been no word from Precious and Suze since our strained first meeting at the shopping mall on Christmas Eve. We'd gone for a pizza and Precious had barely said a word, leaving Suze to cover her silences. The problem was we'd rapidly exhausted the subject of school and there was little else to say.

We'd said our goodbyes without arranging to meet again and I'd gone home sobbing, blocking them both on social media. We hadn't messaged for weeks and I had another life now, one without room for either of them in it. They hadn't given me Christmas cards, saying they'd rather give money to charity, thanking me for the cards I'd sent and for the perfume I'd bought them, a waste of money and energy. Their loss! I'd been given cards and lovely gifts from my roommates at Helton Manor, and had a sexy, American boyfriend. What did they have? They hadn't shown any interest in that snippet of news and I'd suspected a hint of jealousy.

@LordBob from Pictapost was also at the back of my mind. It was thanks to what had happened between us at the Christmas party that I'd summoned up the confidence to meet Danny, ready and willing for the same experience and excitement. I was unlikely to ever see Robert again. Apart from the roses, he'd sent me some really nice messages on Pictapost that caused me to blush and he swore he hadn't been boasting. His profile was full of photos of him and a beautiful blonde girl, a steady girlfriend, and I was surprised at how envious I was. I often daydreamed of the night we had together and that was more important to me than him cheating on this girl. I had no regrets at all. I took his flowers home, telling Mum I'd bought them for her at the coach station and she was chuffed.

Now my focus was on Danny.

I was expecting him to arrive on the third of January. Gran and Granddad were leaving for Ireland on New Year's Day. Granddad was nursing a hangover from the New Year's Eve celebrations and had to be dragged out of bed by a disapproving Gran.

'There's plenty of food in for you, Cherry, love, I did a shop yesterday,' she said, watching the driver pile their cases into the boot of the taxi. 'Your bed's ready and the room's aired, and Cara's next door...'

I laughed and gave her and Granddad a kiss goodbye. 'Thanks, Gran. Now go and enjoy yourselves and say hello to Auntie Maura.'

'Your mum will ring you every morning...'

'...and you'll ring me every evening. You said! Go on, the boat will sail to Dublin without you!'

Finally, the taxi disappeared into the main road.

Yes, they've gone!

My joy bubbling over, I ran into the house to message Danny.

The one fly in the ointment was Cara. She had nothing to do all day but twitch her curtains and spy on the neighbours. She was bound to tell Gran if she saw me and Danny together. I had two days to work out how I was going to get him into the bungalow without her noticing. It was a good job my room was next to an outside wall. Imagining Danny's hands on me and his lips on my skin sent my senses into a quiver of excitement.

Once my grandparents were safely out of the street, I rushed to my room.

'Are you there, my Beautiful Brown-Eyed Baby Boy?'

It was early evening in America and Danny got back straightaway.

'Hi, baby.'

'Hi!'

'Shall we go on video?'

We dialled in.

'Hey, baby, what if we used Zoom? Pictapost is getting rid of its video soon,' he said, 'and shouldn't I have your phone number?'

I hesitated. 'Dunno.'

He laughed. 'I'm coming halfway across the world to see you and you won't give me your number? I need it to tell you I've arrived. If you're not coming to the airport I'll have to get a coach to your town.'

My teeth chattering, I stuttered out the digits. Shortly afterwards, he sent a photo, saying, 'Love to my queen.' I saved his number in my contacts.

'Have – have you booked your flight?'

'I have and it's a long journey, thirteen hours from LA. I have to change twice in Washington and Belfast. I'll be tired; I hope your bed is comfortable, baby.'

I blushed. 'It is. How much was your ticket?

'Around eight hundred dollars,' he sighed, 'a lot of money for a few days stay.'

'I'm sorry,' I mumbled guiltily.

'Baby, it's all good. I scraped the money together and I'm aching to see you. I guess we won't have much chance for sightseeing.'

My body tingled, knowing exactly what he meant. 'No, probably we won't.'

'I'll see you soon, baby. I've got to finish packing.'

Reluctantly, I let him go. In forty-eight hours we'd be together properly at last.

I decided to forget Cara and take the chance she wouldn't see me let Danny into the bungalow and if she did and grassed to Gran and Mum, I'd say he was a gay friend I met in Helton and stayed overnight, sleeping on the couch. He'd be long gone before my grandparents arrived home and if Mum wasn't happy he'd slept over, hard luck. My happiness meant more to me than her getting mad over that.

My head was all over the place on the morning of the third of January and I'd hardly slept the previous night. Was I doing the right thing? What if Danny blew me out? Part of me wanted to bottle the whole thing; the problem was he'd paid all that money for the plane fare. Or had he?

I'll be furious if he stands me up!

I got up at seven and spent the morning wandering around the bungalow like a lost soul, waiting for Danny's call to tell me he'd arrived at the station. The coach was expected to get in around half-past eleven. I jumped a country mile when my phone rang at nine: Mum from Spain enquiring how I was, that I was eating properly and that I was behaving. She rang every morning and I wondered if she was bored at the villa, judging by what she was saying.

'Yes, I am being good.' I was planning to be a very bad girl indeed! 'You can stop ringing me every day, Mum. I'm coping fine.'

'I'm your mother and you're on your own...'

'I'm not, am I? Mrs Fredric is next door and keeps poking her big nose in.'

Cara had been a real pain, knocking morning, afternoon and evening. If I went out to the shop to get some bread she poked her head out her front door.

'She's not that bad, love.'

'Oh, Mum, she's like some creepy unpaid spy. James Bond's got nothing on her!'

'That's unkind, Cherry.'

'Yeah, soz. Fair enough.'

She's a pain in the arse, Mum, and here's why....

Confiding in Mum, to anybody, really, and confessing to Danny's impending visit was a non-starter. I was also uncertain how Tulip might take such a revelation; it was probably for the best she'd gone home to Swansea for the holidays. I stopped short of sending messages to Suki and Rahma because I was embarrassed, and no way was I going to tell Tasha!

'Mrs Frederic goes to see her daughter every week, usually on a Tuesday,' said Mum. 'You'll get some respite from her if she does go today.'

My heart leapt and I tried to hide my joy. 'What time does she go out?'

'She usually leaves in the morning and spends all day there. Why?'

'Curiosity, that's all.'

'What have you got planned today?'

'Nothing. It's pouring out.'

'Give Precious and Suze a call.'

I swerved that particular subject. 'I've got my book and there's a couple of box sets on Netflix. It's a bit cold to lounge round the pool, see!'

'Sarky! You were welcome to join us.'

'Chill your beans, Mum. I won't be bored and I'm glad not to be at school.'

'Speak tomorrow, love.'

'Yeah, 'bye, Mum, the doorbell's ringing.'

Cara stood on the step in her coat, carrying her umbrella and bag. I prayed Mum was right and she was off to her daughter's.

'Hello, Mrs Frederic.' The rain was coming down heavily now and I managed to hide my delight at her departure. 'Are you going out?'

'Yes, love, I'm off to visit me daughter,' she said. 'Tuesday's her day off work. I always go round there for a bit of dinner and tea and to see the grandkids home from school. They're off this week, o' course, and they'll be visiting me on Sunday for their dinner. How are you doing?'

'Good, thanks. If the rain goes off...'

'I think it's on for the day, to be honest, love. Now, I'm off to catch me bus. I'll be back around eight if you need me.'

'Thanks, Mrs Frederic. Hope you have a nice day at your daughter's.'

I waited for her to disappear round the corner, let out a whoop of elation, closed the front door and danced into the living-room, my phone ringtone up full, ready for Danny's call.

Midday slowly approached and I was nearly out of my mind with eagerness and anticipation. I screamed as my phone rang and Danny's name flashed on the screen.

Keep your knickers on, Cherry!

Puffing out my cheeks, I swiped to accept the call.

'Hiya,' I spluttered.

'Baby!' said Danny. 'I'm at the station. Sorry, the bus got in late. Where are you? I was hoping you'd be here to meet me.'

'I – I was waiting for you to call me.'

'Are you coming?'

'Yes, yes.' I opened the Uber app on my phone and quickly chose my cab. 'I won't be long.'

Dressed in the tightest pink top from my wardrobe, jeans and the highest black heels I possessed, I grabbed my bag and keys, tidied my hair, touched up my mascara and lipstick, locked up the bungalow and dived into the taxi. It weaved its way through the town traffic and scared I was going to wet my pants, the first thing I did on arriving at the bus station was to head to the Ladies' toilet. I washed my hands, examined my image in the mirror, brushed my hair, clutched my chest and lifted up my boobs, taking in gulps of air.

'Here goes nothing,' I said to my reflection.

Managing to calm down, I went out into the coach station, pouting and sexy, sauntering along on my heels, my hips swaying seductively and enjoying the attention I was getting from the men I passed. I winked at one of them, an older, dark-haired bloke in a suit, licking his lips at me. *Dirty old man! I'm young enough to be your daughter!* It was all kinds of wrong and delightfully naughty to have such sexual power. Laughing inwardly, I carried on walking. The reaction had boosted my morale.

'Cherry?'

My jaw dropped open and I thumped back down to earth, my world rocked to the core.

'I...'

We stared at one another, me gobsmacked, him grinning like a Cheshire cat. My mind was racing.

Who the hell are you? You're a boy, not a man!

'Hi, baby.'

'You...'

'What?' The voice from the video calls was the same. 'I'm not what you were expecting? *You* certainly are. You're far more beautiful in the flesh.'

He moved in for a kiss on my lips. Sensing my alarm and the heat rising in my body, I recoiled and he missed his target.

'There's no way you have an eleven-year-old daughter!' I burst out. 'You're no older than sixteen and...'

'Can we do this later, baby?' he said. 'I've been on a thirteen hour trip from the States and I haven't slept much. I really need a shower and to sleep for a few hours.'

'Oh, yeah, right.' Fair enough. He'd come all this way and I couldn't send him packing, not now. I had to admit he did look knackered. 'I'll book an Uber.'

It was an uncomfortable ride home. I was stunned, lost for words, and he was obviously tired, using his body to communicate instead, snuggling up to me in the back seat of the taxi and rubbing his hand gently along my thigh, ogling invitingly at me. I froze, biting my lip at the pleasant sensation of his touch giving me goose pimples.

He closed his eyes and I took the opportunity to study him more closely. The scar across his right brow niggled at my brain and triggered an old memory. His skin had a hint of stubble and was smooth and young, giving me the urge to run the back of my hand lightly across his cheek, awakening a craving in me I was ashamed to acknowledge.

The taxi drew up outside the bungalow and I nudged him awake.

'Danny.' Was that really his name? What else was I supposed to call him? 'We're here.'

'Mmm.' He stretched and yawned widely. 'Cool. Lead the way, baby.'

I hope you know what you're doing, Cherry Hill.

Twenty-Four
Adam

I was fully prepared for Cherry's hostile welcome. I'd travelled from Suffolk (ensuring part of my 'journey' included the connection from Heathrow to create the illusion of me arriving from the airport), thinking out my bullshit excuses to convince her I hadn't meant to intentionally deceive her. The stuff I'd bought to help me be persuasive burned a hole in my jeans pocket, and the revealing photos she'd sent me, stored on my phone, were another means of insurance I'd use if I had to. I'd geared up for a feisty rejection, to be called a fraud and a catfish, and to be fair it was probably justified. Yet I firmly objected to the label 'catfish'; catfishers rarely, if ever, revealed themselves in person to the people they victimised. I was nothing worse than a player and fine, a scammer. I'd needled her into giving me money and now I was going to fraudulently get my kicks from her. I was determined to win her round.

Her grandparents' property was on one level: a bungalow-type house similar to the one Scott lived in, much smaller and attached to another dwelling next door. It was homely and spotlessly clean. In the front room the flowered-patterned suite stood on a plain brown carpet and a red rug was displayed in front of the marble fireplace. Cherry led me to her bedroom where there was a single bed and I ached at the expectation of having fun under the pink duvet. Judging by the make-up and deodorant lying on the dressing-table, and the posters of pop bands on the leafy wallpaper, it had been in use for a while.

'This used to be my room and Gran keeps it ready for me,' she explained to break the awkward silence. 'Sorry the bed isn't any bigger,' she added hastily. 'I hope – I hope you'll be comfortable.'

'I'm sure we will be,' I said, reaching for her hand and caressing her fingers.

Biting her lip and running her other hand up and down her arm nervously was strangely seductive. Throwing my rucksack on the bed, I moved closer and took her in my arms. Her body stiffened in my embrace.

'What's wrong, my queen, are you shy?'

'I…' She turned her head away. 'No.'

'Shall we talk?'

'You said you were tired,' she reminded me.

'I am. May I have a shower first? You can soap my back.' She gasped and I smirked, releasing my hold on her. 'I'm teasing. Do you have any food?'

'I'll make you a cheese sandwich,' she stammered, clearly relieved I'd set her free.

'Cool; and I'd love some coffee.'

She led the way to a small dining area off the kitchen. I sat down at the table and watched her prepare the sandwich through the crack in the door, the tightness of her top and jeans stirring a longing for her that astonished me. Five minutes later, wearing a strained expression, she presented the sandwich and a mug of coffee, her fingertips sweeping the table top slowly.

You're not eating?' I said.

'I'm not hungry.'

The drumming of her fingers on the table was beginning to grind my gears. 'What is it, baby? What's wrong?'

'You're not Danny!' she blurted out. 'Danny has an eleven-year-old daughter. You're just some kid! Who are you? What's happened to Danny?'

I bit into the sandwich and replied calmly, 'What are you saying? I *am* Danny.'

She slammed her hand down hard on the table and coffee splashed everywhere. 'You're *not!*'

She shot up from the table and sent her chair flying. I was that shocked at her rage I remained rooted to the chair. 'I am, baby, honestly.'

'Stay away from me!' she screamed, and I was stunned to see her thrusting a knife. I shook my head, trying to hold on to my sanity, whereas in reality my knees were knocking.

'Why did you invite me back? Why not send me away at the coach station?'

Her lip trembled and her arm was unsteady. 'I – dunno...'

'You're not making sense.'

'And you're a complete stranger.'

'You've seen me on video. It was me you spoke to.'

'Y-yeah, but…' slowly, she lowered the knife, keeping tight hold of it, 'I think Ceridwen's right. You've been grooming me. You're not the same person in the photos on Pictapost and no way are you old enough to be anyone's dad. What's going on?'

I was stalling, trying to work out how to combat this intense questioning. 'You trust the word of some troll over me? You haven't told me why you invited me back here if you really do think I'm a fraud.'

She staggered against the upturned chair. 'I – need an explanation.'

'You could have had that at the airport and told me to leave if you weren't satisfied,' I pointed out.

'I was in shock. I reckon you're an impostor and by coming all this way you've put me on the spot...'

I cut her short. 'Do you find me attractive?' Judging by the way she surveyed me shyly from under her long lashes and the flush in her cheeks, she did. 'You do, right?'

She muttered and turned away in confusion.

'That's a yes,' I said triumphantly. 'Why sweat over the difference in real life and in the photos? I'm all yours, baby.'

'No, you're not! Own up, will you, you've been stringing me along over one big fat lie!'

My pulse was racing and I inhaled silently, seeking inspiration to lie my way out. 'I admit I invented a few things. You were expecting a man, not a boy, and I was out to impress you.'

'You're thinner and darker in all the photos,' she blustered.

Think fast, Adam. 'It's the diabetes. The insulin puts weight on me.'

'Does it turn your eyes green and your hair fairer?'

I laughed. '*You're* different to your snaps! Your eyes aren't that blue in real life and you've changed your hair.'

'Mine are blue. You can see they are. There's a big difference between the colour of your eyes and what I see on Pictapost: green in real life, dark brown, practically black, in the photos.' She flicked the screen on her cell. 'There!' I saw the latest photo I'd uploaded to Pictapost, of Petrov at the beach in Los Angeles. 'That's not you, is it?'

'You're right,' I said, holding firm to my story. 'I told you, it's the diabetes.'

'Now explain the change in your eye colour.'

There was no denying it to me or to her: I had no explanation for it. I stood up slowly, wary of the knife she was clutching, gently picked up the chair and set it back on its feet.

'Here, sit down and have a coffee.'

'Not coffee.' She groaned and a tear dropped on her cheek. 'I've got a headache.'

'You're stressed, that's why. You need to drink. Coffee won't be any good for that. Have a glass of water.'

She collapsed in the chair. 'There's a bottle of Coke in the fridge. I'll have that.'

I went into the kitchen and opened the fridge, pulled out the two litre bottle of Coke, already opened, and poured some into a glass from the cupboard. Placing it in front of her, I said, 'Do you need some painkillers?'

Sniffing, she rubbed her hand through her hair. 'There's Paracetamol in the bathroom cabinet.' She was getting ready to stand up.

'No, I'll get it.'

Without objection, she put the knife on the table, took the glass in her hand and sipped the Coke, crying silently now. Abandoning the thought of snatching the knife from her in case she got to it first, I left for the bathroom, finding the Paracetamol packet in the cabinet and returned to the dining-room to find her on her phone.

'No need to fuss, Mum, honestly,' she was saying between sniffs. 'I've got a bit of a cold, that's all.'

Her glass was empty. I mouthed to her, 'Another?' She nodded and continued her conversation. I regained my composure: this was my chance. Luckily, the chair she was sitting on was facing away from the door, meaning she had her back to the kitchen. I placed the glass on the worktop, pouring in more Coke and speedily taking out the small packet from my pocket to add the contents, frequently turning round to guarantee she wasn't looking.

A few moments later, she ended the call and I put the glass in front of her.

'That was my mum,' she said. 'She thinks I sound a bit funny.'

'Funny?'

'Strange. Not myself.'

'And are you?'

She studied the glass of Coke and the two tablets in the palm of my hand.

'I suppose.' She took the tablets, put them in her mouth and swallowed them. Satisfaction and regret swept through me: satisfaction that I was going to prove my heterosexuality and regret that I needed to do something drastic to achieve that. Pushing the shame from my mind, I bent down and kissed her. For a few seconds, I enjoyed a very pleasant thrill, until she pulled away.

'Listen,' I said, 'it's obvious this ain't gonna work out. I'll split back to the States.'

'No,' she said, 'there's no need. If you are the lad I've been speaking to on Pictapost…' She stood up and swayed, putting her hand to her head. 'Oh.'

'What's wrong?'

She collapsed back in her chair. 'D – dizzy.'

I reached for her hand and kissed it. 'Are you gonna puke?' I hoped not, she'd lose what I'd put in her drink. 'Baby, you're sick. Please go and lie down.'

She allowed me to lead her to her bedroom, where I sat her down on the bed. She offered no resistance as I lifted her legs, laid her flat and climbed next to her, putting my hand under her top to caress her and passionately kissed her neck.

'Why did you keep harassing me for money?' she said drowsily.

'I haven't.'

'You said it was – for your – imaginary – daughter.'

'Yeah, sorry, actually she's my sister.'

'Is she?'

It was working. I opened the contents of the other packet in my possession. What a pity it had to be this way.

'Hush now, baby. Come here.' My lips met hers and I set to work.

***

The desire was there on my side at least, to demonstrate my passion for Cherry and to prevent Petrov completely invading my emotions. Cherry drifted in and out of consciousness, moaning at intervals, unaware of events unfolding around her. Afterwards, and ignoring my shame, I adjusted her clothing and left for the bathroom where I showered and dried using the same towel she'd been lying on. I expected her to be out cold and was surprised to see her sitting up in bed, hugging her legs, her head resting on her knees. The towel tied firmly around my waist, I retrieved my clothes from the floor sharpish and noted her paleness.

'What's – what's going on?'

'Remember, baby? I needed to have a shower.'

'Oh.' She nodded slowly. 'Right, yeah. Ooh, I feel woozy.'

'Go and rest a bit more.'

She flopped back against the pillows. 'I'm dead thirsty.'

'I'll get you some water.'

Don't spike her drink again. She'll end up in the emergency room.

She drained the glass. 'Better?' I said.

'Yeah. Where's my phone? I need to ring Mum back, tell her I'm all right.'

'You left it in the dining-room.'

I fetched it and handed it to her. 'Cherry?'

'Yeah?' She glowered at me.

Tell her you're Adam before you chicken out.

I climbed onto the bed, took her phone, nuzzled into her neck and put my arms around her waist, drawing her body close to mine.

'What if I told you my real name begins with the letter A?' I whispered.

Boy A.

Twenty-Five
Cherry

I was in a strange sleep where I imagined I was back in my old bed in my grandparents' bungalow and had no memory of why I was there. I focused bleary-eyed on the familiar wallpaper and pictures. Realising where I was, I sat up slowly, my head aching, my skin hot and clammy and my mind foggy and confused. I must be ill and Gran and Granddad were taking care of me. Yes, that was it; but how come I was dressed? I noticed a glass of water on my bedside table and drained it thirstily, somehow managing to get out of bed, walking dazedly to the door and slowly along the hallway towards the bathroom where I refilled the glass from the cold tap.

'Gran? Granddad? Are you there?'

The telly was on in the living-room and I wondered if they hadn't heard me.

I gaped at him. 'Who – who the hell are you? What are you doing here?'

He was sitting forward on the sofa in front of the telly, tapping on his phone. He jumped up and said, 'Baby? You've been asleep for ages.'

It took me a moment for my brain to register the accent: American, Canadian maybe. Scared now, I backed away and he stepped closer. I repeated my question, adding, 'Where are my grandparents?'

Puzzled, he tilted his head. 'Have you forgotten already? I'm Danny.'

'D-Danny?' Did I know anyone called Danny? 'What have I forgotten?'

I heard the words in my head: *'What if I told you my real name begins with the letter A?* and my mind flipped.

Oh, shit.

Now it was all flooding back like a massive tsunami. Fearing I might faint, I let him put his arm around me and guide me to the sofa, where I flopped down. He raised my legs to lay me flat and put a cushion behind my head.

'Where's my phone?'

'In your room; you were speaking to your mom. Go back to bed, baby, you're bushed...'

'I need my phone!'

'I'll go see if it's there.' A moment later, he reappeared and handed it over. 'Here it is. It was lying at the foot of the bed...'

I snatched it from him and flicked through the images. That scar above his right eyebrow had been bugging me from the moment we'd met at the coach station. My foggy brain was slowly beginning to clear and I recalled seeing a lad on Pictapost, a scar over his right brow. I'd fallen for him and we'd been messaging. Seeing a blond-haired lad in school uniform, recognition stirred: the scar! My hands trembling, I flicked through more photos and came across a picture of a boy, dark-haired, and much thinner than I'd expected.

Danny, and no scar.

'This isn't you, is it?' I demanded, showing him the photo, my senses recovering by the minute. Things were coming back to me and I was ready for a confrontation. 'You're Adam! You told me that scar was caused at a baseball match and the hair never grew back. Tell me what you're playing at! What were your motives for this whole charade?'

How brave of me to challenge him when I was vulnerable: no one but me knew he was here. If he became violent, I was in no position to fight back. He sat down next to me and I purposely inched away.

'I was seriously into you,' he said. He took my hand and I found myself reluctantly melting into him. 'And you were definitely into me.'

'I was.' Why had I admitted to that? 'It was a stupid thing you did.'

'I told you, baby, my account was hacked by...' I caught him staring at my phone where I was examining Danny's picture.

'By him?' I said.

Adam removed his hand and stuttered, 'He's in my class and I chose his snaps at random.'

'Why pretend in the first place and why say you were older?'

A long pause.

'Because of what you did.'

I tried not to show any alarm. 'What did I do to you? I'd never met you before today.'

'I met a pal of yours.'

'What pal?'

He described her. 'She didn't tell me her name,' he finished.

The penny had dropped.

'It *was* you in Helton?' I cried.

'Of course it was, you tried to visit me in hospital,' he pointed out angrily.

'I swear I had no idea it was you.' Not quite true, it had crossed my mind. 'I tried to visit you...'

'To find out if I'd squeal on her?'

I was choosing my words very carefully. 'She was really freaked out by what she did and for what it's worth she was worried you were badly hurt.'

'There was no need for her to attack me, was there?'

'No,' I admitted. 'She did say she recognised you from my Pictapost list. She was thinking of her mate, see.'

'The dead girl, right?'

'Yes. She kept telling me to steer clear of you and the creeps on Pictapost. Why *did* you come and see me in Helton, anyway?'

'I wanted to be the real me, Adam, and not Danny,' he snapped, 'and to pick up where we left off and not pretend any more, get Danny out of your head and me back into it. I hated myself for deceiving you. You said you loved me. That girl got it all wrong. She ruined everything for us and you let her.'

His outburst scared me.

'I'm sorry,' I mumbled.

'You weren't interested in how I was; you were interested in protecting her!'

'I *was* worried, we all were!' I cried. 'Tasha, she's...'

'Is that her name?'

Bollocks! Why did I say that? If he goes to the police and grasses her up... 'She's vulnerable, Adam. Essie's death really upset her. She was trying to protect me. She...'

His kiss prevented me from saying any more. For a few precious moments I was carried away, enjoying the taste of him, and then sense took over: he was lying on top of me and everything became ugly and very real. I pushed him off, visualising more horrible scenes that refused to leave my mind, alarming sensations down below and a nightmare that had really happened. I collapsed onto the carpet and began to hyperventilate.

'Baby, what's wrong?' He moved closer, trying to comfort me, and I shoved him away again. I tried to tell him what he'd done, except the words wouldn't come out.

'Keep calm, baby,' he said. 'That's it. You'll be OK.'

Weak and distressed, I had to allow him to help me. He suggested I went back to my room to lie down.

'No, I...'

'Shall I give you some space? We're both angry. I'll get out of your hair.'

'Where will you go?'

'Home. I'll be late getting back...'

'I need a bath,' I announced, not interested in hearing any more. I'd read somewhere you weren't supposed to bathe and change your clothes for DNA evidence, but I felt dirty and was frantic to wash him from my body.

'Fine, you have a bath and I'll find out the trains from here back to Sudbury.'

Good. Piss off back to Sudbury, wherever that is. Get out of my life!

Right now, I had to lock the bathroom door, not only to keep him out, I also needed the privacy of a locked room, protected by the noise of the running bath taps. Carrying my phone, I retreated to the bathroom, leaving him to find out if there were any trains today.

Instead of ringing the police, I rang Tulip and was irritated her phone went straight to voicemail, so I tried to get hold of Suki. Suki had been round the block and had more experience than I had. First, I left a comment on Ceridwen's latest Pictapost account: 'You were right, he's a fraud.' I logged out and dialled Suki's number, not knowing what time it was in Japan. I kept on the line, willing her to pick up.

'Cherry-chan? Hi! Did you have a lovely Christmas?' I burst into tears and she cried, 'Darling, what's wrong?'

'Oh, Suki!' I gulped. 'I'm in such a mess!'

'Slow down, Cherry, you're scaring me! Take a chill pill and start from the beginning.'

'I'm not disturbing you, am I? What time is it in Osaka?'

'It's gone nine-thirty in the evening. No sweat, I'm chilling out in front of the TV, that's all. My parents are out at a dinner party. What's up?'

I told her everything.

'And he's there now?' she said angrily.

'Yeah.'

'Cherry, you realise what he's done, right?'

'I've no proof, Suki; it'll be his word against mine.'

'You *have* to tell the police. They'll investigate and yeah, it'll be hard...'

'It'll kill my mum! I can't put her through that! It's my fault for contacting him in the first place and for being tricked by him.'

'Oh, rubbish! He was clever, convincing, a fraud and he took advantage of you. He fooled you.'

He also fooled you.

'For now, he needs to be taught a lesson,' she went on. 'How long is he sticking around for?'

'He's trying to find a train now. Hopefully, he'll go tonight; otherwise, I'm kicking him out first thing tomorrow.'

'Hmm. Can you keep him there a bit longer, Cherry?'

'Why? Suki, what are you planning? And what can you do from Osaka?'

'You'll find out,' she said mysteriously. 'Think of an excuse to keep him there. Give me your grandparents' address. No questions, either; Auntie Suki is going to fix this. Let's change the subject. What did you get for Christmas?'

Our conversation over, I put my phone down on top of the toilet seat. Keeping up the pretence and acting all cool around Adam was going to be an almighty challenge. No, I refused to do it. I had to get away from him for good. How was Suki going to organise that?

I soaked and scrubbed to get the smell of him off my body. I was damaged goods now: he'd taken me without my consent. I dried and dressed in my blue jogging bottoms and baggy top and put the clothes I'd been wearing in the washing-machine on a boil wash. Burning them in Granddad's incinerator was preferable and risky; Cara would come round poking her big nose in.

Now to face my demon.

Twenty-Six
Adam

Cherry found me in the living-room deleting another notification from that Ceridwen.

'Hello, my queen,' I said breezily. 'Better now?'

'Yeah. Did you find a train?'

'Nothing doing today, I'm afraid.' I was uneasy. Judging by her behaviour, it was going through my mind she suspected what I'd done. 'There are no coaches, either. I guess I'll have to find some place to stay tonight.'

'That'll be difficult at New Year.' She paused. 'You – you can stay here tonight, I suppose.'

'Oh, baby, I was hoping you'd say that.'

The screams were coming from the kitchen where Cherry was preparing dinner. I ran in to see what was happening, stunned to see two individuals wearing hoodies and balaclavas and wielding baseball bats. Cherry was cowering in the corner of the room, terrified.

'Hey!' I shouted.

Incensed, I grabbed the hot pan from the stove and threw it at one of them, a man, sending him yelling and staggering back against the door.

I was totally unprepared for what happened next.

The noise from an engine and a rocking motion brought me back to consciousness. I was in the back of a moving vehicle, not the trunk of a car, in a van packed full of trash. Moaning, I sat up, trying to figure out what was going on. Suddenly, it came flooding back to me: a hooded figure wielding a baseball bat in my direction and everything going black.

What the absolute fuck was happening here?

At last, I was able to focus more easily and took in my surroundings, noting a couple of chairs stacked in one corner tied together with rope, some cardboard boxes and electrical equipment. Whatever this van was used for was of no interest to me. All that mattered was I'd been bundled into the back of it and was being taken someplace against my will.

And what had happened to Cherry?

I noticed my rucksack and trolley case lying underneath the chairs. Strange that whoever was doing this had brought those along, had gone to a lot of trouble to snatch me and bring all my belongings. Where was my phone! I inched forward, grabbed my rucksack and peered inside: not there, nor was it in the case.

Damn it! Either they've got it or I've left it at Cherry's place!

Stumbling forward, I hammered against the cab yelling, 'Hey! Let me out!' Fifteen minutes later, my throat hoarse and sore and my fist aching, I gave up, hoping I'd be set free once the van came to a halt.

I had no concept of time without my phone and I'd left my watch in my bedside drawer at school. My head was sore and I allowed my imagination to take over, deciding Cherry was behind this. Obviously, she'd realised what I'd done to her and called for help. Had she been genuinely scared those guys barged in? Was this Helton all over again? I put my head in my hands, not knowing what to think, and reflected on the mess I was in now.

Why had I ever fallen for Cherry bloody Hill?

The van slowed and stopped. I braced myself, my pulse racing. Now what? What were they planning to do? Beat me up? Murder me?

The doors flew open to darkness and two people in the same hoodies and balaclavas worn by the men in the kitchen, climbed into the van. I was dragged by the arm and flung onto the grass, my rucksack and case thrown at me. The two individuals jumped out and slammed the doors shut. One of them kicked me hard on the leg, growling in broken English, 'That's for scalding me!'

'Leave it!' said his mate, also in a foreign accent. 'Let's get out of here!'

'Hey!'

What was the point in shouting? The van had already roared off down the dark road, without its lights on, leaving me on the grass next to a clump of trees, a small wood to be exact. It was a dark-coloured vehicle: black, blue, I couldn't tell; no writing on it, no stickers, and the licence plate, if it had one, out of range.

Puffing out my cheeks and counting my blessings that I was alive, I considered my next move and the best direction to go in. I had to get to a phone somehow, get help, perhaps call the police; the problem was there weren't many public phone boxes in the UK; most of them had defibrillators inside and some had been turned into greenhouses and libraries, and was there any point giving the police giving a description of a van when there were hundreds like it in the country?

Tired, wretched, confused and sore, I brushed down my clothes, slung my rucksack over my shoulder and, choosing the opposite direction to the way the van went, dragged my trolley case along, hoping to see another car and hitch a lift. Incensed by the anger and resentment directed solely against Cherry, I ignored the creepiness of the place and focused on revenge. I was done. Convinced she was behind this latest insult, she was going to pay!

Having the immediate problem of getting back to civilisation, coming across lights and houses sent my spirits into overdrive. Forgetting my aches and pains, I hurried along and it suddenly struck me I was on the edge of a place that was kind of familiar: three small cottages, a post office and a shop, not much different to a lot of other small English villages, and spotting *Welcome to West Somerholt* on the sign, I realised I'd been dropped off near The Priory! How come? Cherry must have given the kidnappers the name and location of my school.

Bitch!

And that was Somerholt Wood back there, ancient trees that surrounded the ruins of the old priory from where the school got its name, fenced off from the playing fields and out of bounds to us, unless we chose to break them, which was often. It was unrecognisable to me in the dark and I hadn't really explored the area in detail, coming this way a few weeks ago during a cross country run. My spirits soared. I was five minutes away from safety and I craved food and sleep.

Since some of the boys had returned early from the Christmas vacation, not much was said by the duty staff when I turned up prematurely. Being deprived of my cell, I rang Mom from the phone in the boarding house the next day to lie to her I'd come back to school a few days early and please send on my trunk. She was naturally curious why I was calling her from a landline and I lied that my battery was flat. Next morning, I was told by the mailroom that I had a packet waiting for me in my pigeon hole, minus stamps and postmark, my name written in capitals on the front: ADAM FISHER, THE PRIORY SCHOOL. Wrapped around my phone was a typewritten note: 'Don't contact Cherry Hill again.'

We'll see about that.

They hadn't hacked into my phone. Cherry's photos, including the racy ones, were still there. Amateurs!

I concocted all sorts of crazy schemes for revenge, deciding to do nothing major, not yet. The roses I'd sent to Cherry were a kind of apology for what I'd done and I also hoped they freaked her out. During vacation, there were things to do at school to take my mind off my situation: pantomimes, concerts, soccer, rugby games and walks in dry weather. Meanwhile, my @dannyrob543 account had been closed down for imitating another account and that got me thinking: what if Cherry had found Petrov's real profile and contacted him to say I'd harvested his pics? Thinking of that caused my anxiety levels to rise and they were high enough already.

The new term was fast approaching and the prospect of seeing Petrov again sent my emotions of trepidation, excitement and longing spiralling into madness. Apart from our polite texts on Christmas Day, we hadn't been in regular contact. Even minimal communication at a distance was both unwise and dangerous; a proper relationship was out of the question – and wrong. There was no doubt in my mind now that my encounter with Cherry had done little to quell my attraction to Petrov and if I had another chance…I tried hard to restore control of my senses. Since those fateful few days at New Year, I was constantly comparing Cherry to him and concluded that if I had to give marks out of ten, she'd be a nine and a half and him, off the scale. I loved him that much, ached for him. Cherry had completely left my head and he now filled it in every waking moment.

I encountered Carlton-Greene in the hall.

'How are you, Fisher? Good hols?'

It was the first official day back and I'd gone down to the main hall to see the early arrivals, hoping and dreading to catch a glimpse of Petrov, barely sleeping last night in excited anticipation.

'Yeah, thanks.' I told him a few of the things I'd been up to, missing out Cherry, of course. 'How was your Christmas? Get up to anything exciting?'

'Yeah, it was great.'

He began telling me of all the parties he'd been to, the famous people he'd met, showing me pictures on his phone. Feeling the familiar pleasurable sensation surround me in a thick cloud, I saw my boy in the doorway, his case and rucksack at his feet, cheerfully hugging everyone approaching him. Petrov's gaze fell on me and he rubbed his tongue on his top lip, winking naughtily at me and turning my legs to jelly. I longed to shout out his name, beg him to come to me and take me in his arms. Carlton-Greene's presence faded into the background because my whole attention was focused on the perfection that was Daniil Petrov. The illicit, beautiful reminder of our intimacy stirred within me, shaking me to the core.

'Fisher?' Carlton-Greene was ogling me curiously. 'Are you OK?'

'Sorry, I have to go,' I muttered and ran to the nearest bathroom to empty my churning stomach. Pulling myself together was a colossal effort. I splashed water on my face and glared at my worthless image in the mirror.

Dear God, please get me out of this nightmare!

At some point, of course, we had to meet, sit at the same dining-table and in the same classroom; there was no getting away from him, no ignoring his existence. Another three months in his company loomed and it occurred to me there was a strong possibility of further intimacy between us.

And I might not be strong enough to resist him.

Gradually, I was able to conquer my panic and went back into the hall, where I saw a man in a suit and overcoat showing one of the staff an ID badge, a uniformed police officer standing next to him.

Twenty-Seven
Cherry

Slamming car doors, an engine roaring and wheels screeching almost blocked out the beeping of the oven telling me the meal I'd been preparing was ready, Bolognese and mince bubbling over on the hob. Instinctively, I reached up and turned the button to 'Off'. There was spaghetti plastered all over the floor, kitchen worktop and walls, the result of Adam chucking the pan, also on the floor, at the intruders. I was rooted to where I'd landed on the cold tiles, incapable of movement, until the din of the doorbell brought me back to my senses. Cara shouted through the letterbox: 'Cherry? Are you in there? Cherry! Open the door! I've called the police...'

'Oh, no!' I muttered. The interfering old...! I got up, using the oven to steady my balance and caught my hand on the cooling electric ring. '*Ow!*' I ran to the front door and yanked it open.

'Mrs Frederic, I...'

This small, thin woman, her dyed, black hair failing to hide the specks of grey at the temples and smell from her clothes betraying the human smoking chimney she was, seriously tried my patience and I willed her to go away and mind her own business.

'What's going on?' she cried, pushing her way in. 'I saw people running out of your back door!'

'What people?'

'I heard you scream and saw two men wearing balaclavas from the bedroom window, dragging somebody along your garden path and throwing them in the back of a van. I thought it was you at first. Why were they coming out of your grandparents' place?'

'Call the police and tell them not to come,' I said quickly, trying to remain calm; inside I was trembling. 'I have no idea what you mean; I scalded my hand and dropped spaghetti everywhere, that's all. If you did see anyone, they weren't running out of here.' The hand I'd put on the electric ring was stinging now and I showed her my reddening skin.

'Oh, Cherry...'

It was too late to call off the dogs because already a police car had pulled up and a policewoman emerged from the driver's seat. I refused to let her in and shot her the same line I'd shot a now confused Cara.

'You'd scream if you'd been scalded!' I snapped at the policewoman impatiently, holding my sore hand to my chest to illustrate the point. 'It's a false alarm. You can go now. Thanks for coming.'

'You ought to get that examined,' the policewoman remarked, indicating the burn.

'It's not that bad,' I lied. I'd run my hand under the cold tap and there was no ointment in the house. 'This is all a daft misunderstanding. Sorry.'

'And the report we had of men running out of your house?' pursued the policewoman, pencil poised to write down my answer. Cara finally managed to speak.

'I – may have made a mistake,' she stammered.

'Cara – Mrs Frederic – lives next door,' I chipped in.

The policewoman's glare rested on Cara. 'Are you saying you didn't see two men dressed in balaclavas dragging another man from this property?'

Poor Cara was incapable of a response. For an interfering old busybody, her heart was in the right place and I wished I could explain why I had to lie, that those men had meant business. Sadly, I had to keep my mouth shut otherwise I'd have dropped Suki in the shit. She was definitely behind all this; that's what she'd been planning, to arrange for Adam to be kidnapped and get him away from me. Suki knew all sorts of people. Part of me was torn between admiration for her and pity for Cara, now probably thinking she'd imagined it.

'I'm not making it up,' blustered Cara. 'I *did* see them!'

'I believe her.' I owed Cara that much.

'They were running from your house?'

'No,' I said, blushing, 'I meant if Mrs Frederic saw them.'

The policewoman frowned at me, at Cara, at me again, and back at Cara. 'I'll need a full description of what they were wearing, please.'

She finished giving a vague description of black balaclavas – a balaclava was a balaclava – jackets, jeans, height and build of all three, and a dark van, blue, maybe black, not a clue, and, 'Sorry, no, I didn't see the number plate.' The policewoman nodded, closed her book and put that and her pen in the top pocket of her jacket.

'Right, thanks, that's all for now. I'll knock on your neighbours' doors and see if there are any other potential witnesses. Call us again if they come back and keep all your doors and windows locked, Miss Hill.' She handed me a business card containing her name and mobile number. 'How old are you, sixteen? I'm not entirely certain even at your age you should be here alone...'

'Her Gran wanted me to check on her and her mum rings every morning,' said Cara, relaxing now the policewoman was leaving.

'And my grandparents will be back at the end of the week,' I added.

The policewoman smiled. 'It's good your grandparents have such a kind neighbour. Never mind, Mrs Frederic. It's always best to be on the safe side and we'd rather you contacted us if you see anything suspicious.' She looked up at the roof.

'There's no CCTV, if that's what you're thinking,' I said. 'The neighbours help one another round here.'

'That's right,' said Cara.

The policewoman went to knock on the neighbour's door at the house on the other side of Cara's and Cara said moodily, 'Cherry, I'm sorry if I...'

Impulsively, I hugged her. 'No problem, Mrs Frederic.' Over her shoulder, the policewoman walked away from the neighbour's front door on realising no one was home.

Phew!

'Everyone round here thinks I'm a nosey old cow,' Cara said glumly, 'and I suppose it's true.'

'You're kind and you did the right thing,' I said encouragingly.

'Anyway, I'd better get back to my tea,' Cara said. 'I've got beans on toast going cold on the kitchen table.'

'I love beans on toast.'

'You're welcome to join me. I've got plenty to go round.'

Worcestershire sauce and grated cheese spiced up the beans. In spite of the shock, I was hungry. Cara also had Germolene ointment and a small dressing to put on my blistered hand. I wolfed down the beans on toast and a glass of water, thanked her and went back to the bungalow, pouted at the mess in the kitchen and the hob and suddenly came over nauseous. I ran to the bathroom and threw up the beans on toast.

I needed my bed and alcohol to help me forget recent events. Granddad had a bottle of malt whisky Mum had got him for Christmas. He and Gran had a small drinks cabinet, unlocked; Gran loved the odd gin and tonic. I poured a treble whisky, downing it in one, wincing at the taste and the burn in my throat. I liked the immediate effect it had, not the yucky aftertaste. I staggered to my bedroom and collapsed on the bed.

I woke the next day, my head spinning. A shower did nothing to revive me and I went back to bed, rising late the next morning and recovered enough to have a mug of tea and a slice of toast. The doorbell rang; not Cara for a change, instead a delivery of a dozen, beautiful red roses. Where they really for this address? It wasn't Gran's birthday and it was common knowledge she'd gone away for New Year. They reminded me of the bouquet I'd received from @LordBob. The card read, '*Sorry. A.*'

A for Adam. Boy A.

The next thing I did was to collapse on the floor and weep, dropping the flowers, the events of the last few hours hitting me hard. I'd allowed Adam to do that to me. Whatever Suki had arranged for his punishment, he was obviously safe and alive, sending bloody roses. To think they came close to excusing what he'd done!

My hysteria spent, I recoiled at the carnage of dead blooms on the carpet, a frenzied murder of pathetic green stems and bloody petals everywhere. Panting, I was suddenly sad I'd taken my anger out on the roses, undoing the florist's careful, skilled work. If I ever got my hands on Adam Fisher…!

I forced myself up and stumbled into the kitchen in search of the dustpan and brush kept under the sink, ignoring the un-cleared spaghetti Bolognese on the floor, walls and cooker hob. The bin men were due the next day and the evidence would be gone, but if

Cara brought up the men she saw at the bungalow there'd be tough questions.

Once I'd cleared up the remains and disposed of the body, I went back, sobbing pitifully, to my room to lie down again, putting a pint of water by my bed and a bowl on the floor to catch possible explosive projectile vomiting. Ruining the carpet and the bed, facing another massive clean-up operation and the inevitable explanation to my grandparents weren't an option.

Vibration and buzzing was coming from my jeans' pocket. I pulled out my phone and the screen lit up.

'Hello. Suki,' I said tonelessly.

'Cherry! I've been trying to get hold of you!'

'Have you? Sorry, I haven't checked my calls.'

I'd missed ten, including one from Tulip. I texted her to apologise and promised to call her later.

'Yes. I had to make sure you were safe now Adam's gone.' Suki was acting callously upbeat and maybe I ought to have been a bit more grateful…

'Who were those men and how did they know where to find me and Adam?'

'Friends of friends,' was her evasive statement. I imagined her tapping her nose. 'You told me your gran's address. Relax: the little shit is unharmed. They were merely instructed to scare him and dump him back at that school of his. The baseball bat was insurance. Cherry, you're not bothered, are you? He's not worth it, the sack of trash.'

'He is, yeah…'

I'd rather you'd killed him – no, that's unkind!

'You're depressed,' Suki went on. 'Of course you are. That's why I tipped off the police.'

That brought me up short. Police visits to the Hall and school, my family and everyone else hassling me to tell all, intimate examinations, solicitors, barristers, court appearances...no way was I going to put my mum through all that!

'You did what!'

'I mentioned the drugs, nothing else. *You* have to tell them the rest, darling. You mustn't let him walk away from this, he needs to be punished.'

'I'm not planning to.'

'Good.'
'It's just...'
'What?'
What will it do to my mum?

Twenty-Eight
Adam

They'd had an anonymous tip-off (from Cherry, I guessed) that I was in possession of drugs, conducting a search of my locker, my bag and my dorm cubicle and, in Matron's presence, questioning me in her office.

I was more surprised than they were they found nothing. The dope had definitely been in my rucksack; where was it now? Had it dropped out?

They did find the train and bus tickets and questioned why I went to Cherry's hometown during the New Year. I gave them the same story I'd fed my parents: I'd been visiting a buddy and luckily they bought it, leaving them nothing else to ask. After half an hour, they went away and I exhaled slowly, thankful I'd come through the ordeal in one piece.

Of course, my classmates were intrigued by the police interrogation, firing questions and passing rumours, and I was cornered by a tearful Petrov in the bathroom.

'What have you done, Adam?'

'Nothing, I swear.'

You'll hate me if I tell you the truth!

'The police have been questioning you. Why?'

'It's a misunderstanding. Honestly. I can't bear seeing you so upset.'

I took his hand, raised it to my lips and kissed it, all my doubts subsiding in that one moment. I'd crossed the line and there was no going back. Gently, he put his hand on my neck, drew me to him, kissed me and led me into one of the cubicles, and this time, I had no regrets.

***

A few days later, the expected and inevitable summons to Crane's office came and I stood in front of his desk, hands behind my back.

'So, Fisher, here we are again,' he began, sitting forward and frowning at me.

'Yes, sir,' I said, feigning innocence.

'You're a suspect in the possession of illegal drugs and have been questioned by the police. You can imagine my uneasiness. I'm afraid I had to phone your parents to inform them. They're both very disappointed.'

Shit.

'The cops found nothing...'

'Why? Did you get rid of the evidence?'

'I - no!' *I lost it, you moron.*

'Why did you go to Milborne?'

The cops must've told him.

'Surely that's my business? I went to visit a pal and I told my parents the same. There's nothing you can say, I was on vacation.'

'Your mother said it was someone from The Priory and none of our pupils live in Milborne.'

I was angry now. 'I have a lot of buddies outside of this place and I repeat I was on vacation.'

Crane went red. 'Don't be impertinent, Fisher. It makes no difference. You've brought the school into disrepute by inviting a police interview and there's no smoke without fire. I've phoned your mother and she'll be waiting for you at Sudbury Train Station.'

'You're suspending me again?'

'No, Fisher. You're permanently excluded. A prefect is on his way to take you to your dorm for you to pack your belongings. Your trunk is waiting for you there.'

I swayed on my feet and had to hold the back of the chair for support. Crane creased his forehead in a frown.

'It's been coming for months, Fisher. You were warned: I told you, another strike and you're out. That strike has happened and now you have to leave, the third boy to be excluded from The

Priory in fifty years. An unenviable achievement that won't do your future prospects any good.'

If Crane was worth going down for, I'd have grabbed him by the throat and choked the life out of him, to add murder to my other crimes. My hands gripped the back of the chair, turning my knuckles white. Mom, Dad, and Petrov flooded my head and sent my emotions all over the place.

'It'll kill my mom!'

'That will teach you to think over the consequences of your actions in future, won't it?' A knock at the door interrupted him. 'Come in! Ah, Kwei-Armah.' A Sixth-Former wearing a prefect badge on his lapel entered. 'Please escort Fisher back to Stanthorpe and wait for him to empty his lockers and pack his effects. He leaves us today. A taxi is on its way to meet him at the door in half an hour.'

Kwei-Armah raised his eyebrows slightly at Crane, not disguising his surprise. 'Yes, Mr Crane. Come on, Fisher.'

That was that. I was off, leaving, going for good. There was nothing more to be said. Crane had ruined my mother's life and any prospects I had of securing a real relationship with Petrov. My head was all over the place. Mixed with the dread of facing Mom and Dad was the anguish of how Petrov was going to take the news. Angry and frightened, I left the office without a backward glance.

Outside, Kwei-Armah said, 'You've been booted? What have you done? Is it 'cos of that visit from the fuzz?'

I failed to comment, and throwing my stuff angrily into my trunk, I kept my mouth shut. It was lucky that classes were going on, allowing me to avoid all the expected, awkward questions from my classmates. I'd dreamt and longed for this moment for months and now it had come down to it I was mortified: Mom's distress was one reason, my attachment to Petrov another, and a third was that the school had become a kind of dysfunctional home and family. Mom was going to be distraught and my schooldays were ruined; another black mark chalked up against that slut Cherry Hill! Every event that had led up to this moment was down to her and to think I'd wasted my money on sending her those roses!

'Kwei-Armah?'

'What?'

Not one word had passed between me and my escort during the half-hour I was clearing out my locker, he'd been busy surfing his phone.

'I must say goodbye to the others.'

And especially to Petrov.

'Everyone's in class,' Kwei-Armah pointed out.

'Yeah, it's Geography now.'

'And you're planning to gate crash the lesson and announce you're offski?'

I nodded.

Kwei-Armah chortled. 'I reckon it won't hurt. You're already dead meat and have nothing to lose. I'll wait for you.'

Back in the main school building, I found the classroom and barged in.

'Now can anyone tell me – Fisher!' I was surprised to see Miss Emerson standing in front of the class. Geography was usually Mr Dangerfield's remit. Wait, he was off sick. 'What are you doing here?'

'Weren't you expecting me?'

What does it matter if I'm rude now?

'Miss?' said Aziz in surprise. 'Fisher's not that late…'

'I'm leaving,' I blurted out, fixated on Petrov. 'I've come to say goodbye and good luck to everyone. It's been – an – experience knowing you all.'

A crashing chair broke the deafening silence and everyone jumped.

'Leaving?' Petrov was on his feet. 'What are you saying? Where are you going?'

I choked on my words. Petrov betrayed shock, pain and anger, causing my stomach to churn, and it hit me hard that the brief love affair we'd shared was over for good. My emotions were on the floor; I was going to miss him badly. I was also sorry to say goodbye to Aziz, one of the few people at the school I was able to call an ally.

'Fisher's moving to the day school near his father's air force base,' said Emerson in a strange, over-loud manner. 'Isn't that right, Fisher?'

It was clearly a well-rehearsed explanation and probably not far from the truth if no other options were available for me to continue my education.

'Er…'

Carlton-Greene piped up, 'This is all a bit sudden, isn't it, Fisher? What's up, are your parents strapped for cash and can no longer afford the school fees?'

'Shut up, CG!' hissed Aziz.

Petrov flopped back on his chair in disbelief, his chest heaving, clearly agitated.

Everyone crowded round and Emerson protested at them declaring their amazement and curiosity at my sudden departure. Aziz's voice rose above everyone else's, demanding if the police visit meant I'd been excluded and at that point I decided it was wise to leave. I slammed the door behind me, cutting short Kwei-Armah's phone call.

'I'm ready to go,' I said, and we went along the corridor to the exit without anticipating any further issues, such as half the class in pursuit, for instance. I tried to take no notice of Emerson calling them back, threatening detention and visits to Crane's office.

A hand clutched my arm and I turned to see Petrov focused on me, full of distress.

'Is it true?'

I nodded miserably, grasping his other hand, scared to let go. My spine tingled, both of us painfully aware this was our last meeting; from that moment he was a celebration of a glorious memory I had to push to the back of my mind. He'd been a teen's amazing experiment, like smoking a joint; been there, done that, bought the T-shirt. The anxiety over my sexuality had brought me to this point. I imagined his fury if he ever found out I'd been using his photos to scam a girl and concluded yeah, it was for the best that I was leaving.

'Whatever it is you've done,' he said softly, rubbing his fingers on mine and sending my body into raptures, 'it doesn't matter. I'll always…'

Our beautiful moment was disturbed by Aziz brushing him aside and hugging me. I accepted his embrace reluctantly, whilst concentrating on Petrov's torture.

'You'll be missed, man,' said Aziz sadly. 'Good luck.'

'If you've been excluded, Fisher, tell us why,' added Carlton-Greene slyly, nevertheless extending his hand. I took it, thinking I might even miss him.

Kwei-Armah ended the fond goodbyes by disentangling me from the group, telling them truthfully my taxi was due to arrive. Behind me, Emerson was trying to chivvy everyone back to class. They all obeyed, except Petrov.

'I love you,' he mouthed and I struggled to keep my composure.

'And I love you,' I murmured back.

'Petrov, will you come *on!*' snapped Emerson. He raised his hand briefly to me before allowing her to usher him into the classroom, the door slamming on my world at The Priory, and on the boy I would cherish to the end of my days.

Twenty-Nine
Cherry

You stupid cow, Cherry Hill!

I dropped my phone on the bed, wanting to kill him! I'd willingly sent him those revealing pictures and he was threatening to share them with my entire Pictapost list! My hands unsteady, I notified the moderators and blocked his @dannyrob543 account, immediately receiving a message from a @madhake.

'I've followed everyone on your list,' it read. 'Unless you pay me three hundred dollars I'll send them those snaps.'

'Fuck off!' I typed straightaway, again reporting and blocking. The bell rang for first lesson, meaning I had to wait for break until logging in to see if he'd carried out his threat. It was no surprise I was unable to concentrate on Spanish class and Señor Gonzalez gave me detention and extra prep. Break came and I logged back into Pictapost, getting the shock of my life: another account had been set up and had sent the picture of me in the bathroom to my entire list, the one where I was astride the chair in my bra and pants. I was terrified and on hearing shouts of laughter in the common-room, I turned to see a group of girls gathered round a smartphone and grinning at me. One of them was Clarissa Cleverly and she called over some other girls to show them. Suki and Tasha burst into the common-room, snubbed everyone, grabbed my arms and dragged me out into the corridor, slamming the door on the mirth. Suki raised her phone and there was the photo of me, in the bathroom, on the chair, in all my shameful glory. Rahma came up, her hands on her mouth, her shock obvious.

'Recognise this?' Suki barked in disgust. 'What the hell were you thinking, Cherry?'

Suddenly, I was gulping for air, collapsing on my knees and from somewhere within me came a scream, and another and another.

Blubbing uncontrollably, I puked and ended up in the san, in some sort of sedated state, hearing people talking: Suki, Rahma, Tasha; and Matron saying sternly, 'Clear off, you three. She isn't up to visitors at the moment and the doctor is on his way. Get out from under my feet!'

And Tasha crying, 'It's Essie all over again!'

I must have dropped off, haunted by words such as: *obviously suffered a severe mental trauma; unresponsive; prime candidate for admission to a CAMHS unit*… That must have been the doctor…and: *social media; Pictapost; catfishing; poor, poor child*…

That was Miss Panesar, sounding more troubled than angry. The next person I heard was very familiar. By now, I was awake and staring up at the person I loved most in the world. Mum was holding my hand. I saw through the window blinds that it was daylight and the weather grey and gloomy. The clock on the wall said it had gone twenty-five past two. For a moment, I wondered why I was there, until it all came flooding back to me: Pictapost. Adam, Danny, those awful photos of me and making a show of myself by losing it outside the common-room. The stress was intense.

'What are you doing here, Mum?' I croaked. She was unlike the grand Lady Milborne I'd reluctantly grown accustomed to and was how she used to be, no make-up, her hair tied back in a pony-tail, wearing denim jeggings, white trainers and a ruby-coloured hoodie top.

'I've come to take you home, love.'

'Why? Have I been kicked out?'

'No. I think you're better off back at your old school, where you were happy.'

'I'm happy here now, Mum. I've settled down, got mates.'

She bristled. 'How can you be happy and do – that?'

'I'm sorry, Mum.' I began to sniffle. 'I was lonely at first, see...'

'Say no more, darling. We'll do this at home.'

Back to Milborne Hall and pervy Greg and his equally pervy son. An explanation as to why living under the same roof as Greg was out of the question and she was unlikely to believe me, anyway.

'Won't he be hacked off if I leave Helton?'

She tucked my bedclothes around me in silence. Matron came in bearing a tray of two cups of tea and a wholemeal sandwich. 'It's nice to see you awake and chatting to your mum,' she said, putting the tray down on the table. 'I've brewed you both a cup of tea and will you please try this, Cherry? You haven't eaten for three days.'

She helped me to sit up and arranged the pillows behind me while I grimaced at the cheese sandwich, but my mouth was dry and the tea was very welcome. Mum said, 'Thank you,' for her tea and took a sip.

'Is that how long I've been here?' I took a small mouthful of the sandwich, put it on the plate and pushed it away.

'Yes.' Matron pouted at my rejection of the food and removed the plate.

'Did you call the doctor? I heard things being said; they're sending me away to a looney bin, aren't they?'

Matron cleared her throat and said nothing. Mum replaced the cup on the saucer and said firmly, 'That won't happen, love. You need space at home, that's all.'

'Have you finished your tea, Lady Milborne?' queried Matron briskly.

'Oh, yes. Thanks.' Mum gave up the cup and saucer and Matron carried them to the sink.

'I'd better be off, love, let you get some rest.' Mum reached for her bag and coat hanging behind the chair, stood up, bent down and kissed me. 'I'm staying in the hotel up the road. I'll pop in and see you tomorrow. Goodbye, Matron.'

I was afraid to bring up the subject of going home, in case it reminded her of what she'd said. She found Suki, Rahma and Tasha waiting outside the door.

'Oh,' she said in surprise. 'Hello. Are you here to see Cherry?'

Matron strode to the door. 'What are you girls doing here? You're supposed to be in class.'

'It's the Wednesday half-day monthly staff meeting, Matron,' said Rahma politely.

'Is it, really?' said Matron sarcastically. 'Karen's there in my place. What, did you think you'd sneak in and see Cheralyn without me noticing?'

'Oh, Matron...'

'*Please*, Matron,' I said, handing her the tray, 'can they come in? For five minutes?'

'Now, Cherry...'

'Oh, it won't do any harm, surely?' said Mum impatiently. 'It will give her the opportunity to say goodbye.'

'Goodbye?' echoed Suki, a frown clouding her pretty face. 'What's going on?'

'Suki, mind your manners!' warned Matron.

'Matron,' said Mum coldly, 'I'm giving them permission to come in.'

She blew me a kiss and nodded to the girls on her way out. Infuriated, Matron stood aside and they flung themselves at me, catching me in a collective hug.

'Cherry! Oh, Cherry, how are you?'

'We have missed you!'

'We sent you texts. Did you not get them?'

'I – no...' Where *was* my phone? I found out later Mum had it. Thank heavens I had a password on it to keep her from seeing Danny's photos.

'You poor thing! You look awful.'

'That's right, Tash, cheer her up!' Rahma huffed at her. 'Was that your mum, Cherry? She's nice. What did she mean by goodbye? Are you going home for a bit?'

Three pairs of eyes turned to me for information. There was no point beating around the bush, I told them straight out what Mum had meant.

'What the fu..!' began Suki. Rahma nudged her sharply to remind her Matron was in the room. 'Why?'

'Because of – what happened,' I said lamely.

'I can't say I blame her,' said Tasha.

'You were catfished, Cherry,' said Rahma. 'It happens to people all over social media. You're not the first and you won't be the last. Your mum doesn't get that.'

'Has it ever happened to you, Rahma?'

'No...'

'You're not to blame for any of it, Cherry!' said Tasha. 'That's what – I kept saying – to Essie. She was a victim and – oh, Cherry! You should have listened to me!'

'Tasha-chan!' cried Suki.

'I warned her, Suki...'

'Christ on a bike!' Suki planted her head in her hands in despair.

'Suki, come on, Tasha's right.' I gripped Tasha's hand tightly. 'I was stupid and naive. It's my own fault, and that's why you're angry.'

'I'm angry 'cos I care, you silly cow!' said Suki.

'I – *we*,' Tasha indicated Suki and Rahma, 'were out of ideas on how to help poor Essie. I began to see the signs in you and was desperate to nip it in the bud.'

'And I ignored all the warnings and now I'm in this mess,' I admitted. 'You don't have to remind me, Tasha. I suppose everyone's laughing at me and passing those photos round on social media.'

Clarissa Cleverley, for instance.

'No, they're not,' said Rahma. 'Honestly, Cherry, I'm speaking the truth. I won't tell you what Clarissa said and she was told to keep her trap shut. Everyone's been really worried.'

I almost chickened out of the next question. 'What has Panesar said?'

'Not much,' said Suki. 'There was an assembly and she said if she found out the photos were being passed around there'd be exclusions. You can imagine the faces in the audience!'

'She's going to bin me, I suppose,' I said dejectedly. 'I see now. She's spoken to Mum and that's what Mum really meant by taking me home and sending me back to my old school.'

Rahma shook her head glumly.

'Bottom line is,' Suki leaned back in the chair, 'Panesar knows stopping us using social media will cause a riot and be in breach of our rights. Everyone goes on Pictapost, even the staff.'

'I tell you what she'll do,' said Tasha sceptically, 'she'll make the prefects to go round doing phone and tablet spot-checks.'

'Yeah, and I said it won't work. That's basically spying, and Panesar needn't pretend the prefects aren't using social media, either...'

'Right, you lot,' said Matron, 'your five minutes are up.'

'Oh, Matron, we've hardly had time to tell Cherry a thing!' protested Suki.

'Cheralyn is tired and needs rest.'

I'd been happy to see them, but Panesar and the possibility of exclusion niggled at me and I wasn't in the mood to be sociable any more, at least not then.

'May we visit tomorrow, please, Matron?' begged Rahma.

'Oh, yeah, let them, Matron!' I said. Tomorrow I was sure I'd be in a better frame of mind.

'Very well,' agreed Matron reluctantly. 'For five minutes during afternoon break; and now, goodbye!'

She shooed them out of the door and closed it firmly behind them.

I was instructed to lie down and try to sleep, eventually waking up to the clock showing five-fifteen and Matron standing over me with a tray bearing a bowl of soup and a glass of milk.

'Eat up,' she said cheerfully. 'Then you can have a wash. Miss Panesar is coming to see you.'

Thirty
Adam

Military school in the US, Dad said, to teach the boy discipline; no, snapped Mom, the local secondary school, poorer than it was in comparison to The Priory, was the best option, for me to come home every afternoon and be under their thumb. Thanks to Dad's superiors refusing to pay for military school fees, I was glad Mom won the day. Even so, to expect me to go to school without a phone was both unfair and unrealistic.

'Mom, I'm gonna need a cell,' I protested. 'What if there's an emergency and I need to call home?' I was almost sobbing. It had been four weeks since I'd left The Priory and although I had no cause to have a go at Mom and Dad for being pissed off, they were unfair carrying on the silent treatment this long. The first thing Mom had done on meeting me off the train was to confiscate my phone. Thankfully, she had no knowledge of the scamming and thank God I'd deleted Petrov's photos. It had almost killed me doing that and I hoped his pics were retained in the cloud somewhere for me to retrieve later. Cherry's pics had been removed, too. 'And Scott and Dean? We keep in touch through social media.'

'Not any more,' she said firmly. 'From now on you can use the landline to phone them...'

'It'll cost a fortune!' Had she completely lost her mind? 'What if I email instead?'

'You won't have access to your laptop.'

'Oh, come on, Mom…!'

Dad intervened. 'You gotta be reasonable, honey. The boy will need a phone and a laptop for his schoolwork.'

'He can use the laptop for school if he has to and that's all,' Mom conceded. 'His phone and tablet, however…'

My mood dropped to the floor.

'I'm going to put in a new SIM in your phone and register it in my name,' she told me. 'I'll also re-register your tablet and laptop and install all the social media apps, create my own accounts and put a child lock on all your devices to prevent you from logging on without me getting alerts.'

I gaped blankly at her, inwardly seething.

'It's for your own good, Adam. That Pictapost got you into a lot of trouble and those drugs...'

'There were no drugs, Mom!' I lied.

Again, she stated I hadn't been excluded from school for no reason and that she was waiting for a knock on the door from the cops at any moment. Every day I lived in fear of it. There was no point arguing and trying to find out if what she was intending to do would work. I was pissed off; the phone was new and an early Christmas gift from Dad. I still had my old cell and planned to get a battery for it, or buy a new, cheaper one, a burner phone. I was determined, somehow, to bring Cherry down the best way possible, by exposing her online and giving her hell, and for that I needed access to the 'net.

I had no choice but to accept Mom's judgement. I was due to become a student at the local school the next semester and, in the interim, I was to have a tutor, Janine, a friend of Mom's, to keep my nose to the grindstone. I was glad Mom was too busy to home school me. The evenings and weekends in her company were bad enough without having to suffer her disapproval all day. Forgiveness was overdue; and there was no point requesting to be sent to a school in the States, they'd say no.

These were the worst days of my life. I was fed up and held Cherry responsible for my predicament. I prayed the secondary school gave me a new lease of life and new pals. The problem was semester was weeks away and I remained lonely and isolated. I missed social media and Scott and Dean, and I also longed to gaze at Petrov's photos and posts. The fact I had some respite from that idiot Ceridwen was scant consolation.

On top of all that, there was always the chance the cops could come knocking. My mind was made up: I had to get away from this place, start anew.

The United States was home, not some cold, impersonal air force base in a country I'd never settled in. I was sixteen, old enough to travel alone and I decided I was going back to New Jersey.

First things first: Saturday afternoon, get a replacement phone using dough from my savings during a visit to town on an errand for Mom. Next, buy a one-way plane ticket to the States. I had enough saved in my bank account and searched for a cheap flight on my new phone. The e-ticket landed in my mail inbox straightaway and it suddenly became real. No changing my mind now. I was going to a buddy I trusted, to Scott's. His family owned a ranch and let out cabins to rent on their land for vacations. Lessons over for the afternoon, Janine went home and Mom hadn't returned from work, I sent Scott a Whatsapp to tell him what I was planning and he replied straightaway.

'Dude! What's going on over there! Is it really you? Why have you got a different number?'

I had no chance to type back: Scott was ringing.

'Adam,' he said, 'it *is* you. What the fuck, man? I've been texting, ringing, Whatsapping, Pictaposting, and you went off radar. I imagined all sorts had happened to you.'

'It has. Listen, Scott, I'll tell you everything when I see you, Mom's due home any minute. Can you put me up?'

'Yeah, no problem, you can bunk down in one of the cabins.'

'Great!'

'It's out of season and not many are being rented at the moment. You'll be safe and no one will bother you. I'll fetch you food and stuff and you can figure out what to do later. Hey, Adam, is it really that bad?'

'Yeah,' I said, 'and not all of it's my fault. Scott, it's kind of a long story to share over the phone…'

'OK. What date are you coming?'

'February fourteenth. I land at Newark at four-thirty in the afternoon.'

'Great, I'll skip school and pick you up.'

'Are you sure?'

'No sweat. I'll leave early and tell them I'm going to the dentist.'

My spirits soared; liberty was within reach. Meanwhile, life dragged on at the base as usual and I soldiered on. Janine was a welcome distraction and I enjoyed her lessons. Gradually, Mom and Dad began to thaw towards me and this was why:

'Adam,' said Mom one evening at dinner and sending a glance at Dad, 'your dad and I have been thinking of seeking help for you, for all of us.'

Mom was a great cook and we were eating her famous cottage pie, a dish I enjoyed; suddenly, however, I was robbed of my appetite.

'Help?'

'Yes. We've found a family counsellor.'

'Your mom thinks we'll all benefit from therapy,' added Dad, 'to understand and find out why we do the things that we do, especially you.'

I grimaced at them.

'I've let you down,' I said. 'I get it.'

'It's your exclusion from The Priory,' said Mom, 'and everything else. You haven't been happy in the UK. We – *I've*,' she corrected, 'put pressure on you to be the person you're not. It's my fault you're the way you are. You're used to the American way of life and we ought to have sent you to a school in the US.'

'Mom...'

'No, let me finish.' She put her fork down. 'I've been selfish, love, trying to change you. You were born in New Jersey and went to elementary school there. You have a British mother and an American father; to all intents and purposes, you're American, at least by birth. This is all on me, Adam, sending you to The Priory...'

Her misery tore at my soul. 'Mom, you should have said!'

'We also need to find out why you did what you did,' said Dad. 'Why you needed to turn to drugs...'

'There were no drugs!'

I gave Cherry drugs, there's a difference.

'We've paid for a series of five weekly sessions,' Mom added. 'The first appointment is next Tuesday.'

And that was that.

***

It was an embarrassing experience, sitting in the therapist's consulting room between my parents, listening to Mom's stuttering reasons between sobs for seeking family counselling and Dad ranting over my various wrongdoings. I slouched in my chair and willed the floor to open and swallow me up. It was all about them and horrible for me to have to sit through this decimation of my character. Soon the therapist turned to me. 'Adam?'

Humera was an attractive young British Afghani woman of twenty-three or four. 'Some clueless degree kid who hasn't lived a proper life, nor had a relationship, and probably has no first-hand experience of family problems,' Dad described her. Despite his misgivings, Humera was kind and sensitive.

'I'm sorry for the – disappointment and trouble I've caused,' I said flatly.

'Can you elaborate on that?'

I clammed up and shook my head. My mind was in a confused whirl; all the things I'd done wrong and also the events that had prompted me to do that wrong span round in my head: the veiled bullying at school, my sexuality, and especially Petrov. My shame prevented me from revealing that, not to a young female therapist and certainly not to my parents, not now, not ever. All my focus was on my trip to the States and my goal of freedom.

'We'll leave it there for today,' said Humera at last. 'I'll see you all next week.'

We shook hands, thanked her, and left.

The next two sessions were more open and I found the courage to say a bit more. I admitted to the taunting at school and that my classmates called me The Colonial. Mom and Dad were shocked: why hadn't I told them?

'I rode it out,' I assured them. Petrov hacking my phone and Cherry's photo being passed around fuelled Dad's anger against the Russian nation all over again and the boy I'd locked away in my heart forever, whose very existence haunted my dreams every night.

Does he ever think of me?

It was a white lie that the humiliation of the suspension from school had preyed on my mind for this long, sorry as I was for the hell I'd caused my parents; I remained convinced I shouldn't have been sent away from The Priory in the first place. At the end of our third meeting, we said goodbye and remorse set in, for this was my last appointment. I'd begun to secretly pack my things, stashing my trolley case at the back of my closet, intending to carry the minimum of luggage on my journey; what else I needed I'd get in the States and I planned to find a job to add funds to my savings.

The night before I was due to leave, my nerves were shot and I gave up on sleep, regret goading my mind. At two in the morning, I wrote a goodbye letter, informing Mom and Dad I'd gone away and was safe; it was the kind thing to do. Of course, I anticipated them calling the cops to bring me home from the airport, the first place they were likely to search. It was a good job I'd purposely booked an early morning flight in an attempt to avoid discovery. If there were no delays, take-off was at seven-eighteen. I planned to be at London City airport by six and to get an Uber in the town at four-fifteen. At four I was ready to go, rucksack and case packed, and the letter on my pillow for Mom to find in the morning.

I took a last look round at the room that had been my own space and sanctuary, even if it wasn't much. Letting out a sniff and gulping back a sob, I crept out, pausing outside my parents' room. I put my hand against the door, whispered goodbye and apologised for all the sorrow I'd caused.

An air force base operates 24/7 and unfortunately most of the personnel knew me and my dad. I had no choice, I had to walk out through the gate and show my pass. I had to think up a good excuse how I was going to explain away the rucksack and trolley case. It was bound to attract attention that I was leaving this early in the morning and for somebody to mention it to Dad.

'You're a bit eager to be getting back to that school of yours, ain't ya, bud?' said the guard at the gate, whose name always escaped me.

A voice calling from the office saved my bacon. 'Hey, Grayson, call for you.'

Grayson groused and retreated to take the call, giving me the opportunity to take control of my unease and walk casually through the gate towards the town and to my new life.

Thirty-One
Cherry

I was back at Milborne Hall, planning to return to Helton Manor next term, hoping everything had blown over and be yesterday's news. Suki, Rahma and Tasha had written a touching letter to Mum begging her to reconsider her decision to take me away. I was touched by their words: 'Cherry is one of us. She's our friend and we'd hate to lose her. Everyone loves her.'

Tears of happiness threatened. Even Clarissa Cleverley had signed the card and contributed to the beautiful bouquet of flowers the class had sent me: pink, white and purple blooms sat proudly in a glass vase on a table in the corner of the sitting-room and lasted for weeks.

'What a lovely letter,' said Mum. 'It's a good job I'm not leaving Greg now, isn't it? Otherwise, you going back to Helton will be out of the question.'

It had been somewhat of a shock learning how quickly she'd regretted her marriage, how going up in the world, being Lady Milborne and having money and nice clothes had done nothing for her at all, and how she'd realised early doors of her big mistake.

'You should have said, Mum,' I'd told her. 'You needn't have gone through all this on your own.'

She'd shrugged. 'It's no big deal. I'm not sure I ever really liked him, to be honest. I was flattered by the attention he paid me, that's all. He was there and…'

'So why marry him?'

I was pissed off. There'd been no need for her to go through with it; he'd perved at me and sent me away. That said, if she didn't love him, I was optimistic she'd dump him in the future.

She sniffed. 'For his money, love, we were on our uppers and needed the security.'

'You had a job and the cottage.'

'Jobs don't last forever these days, love.'

'Has he ever told you he loved you?'

'No. Greg hasn't got it in him to love anyone except himself. All that can be said of him is that he's good to me. I'm using him and he's using me. That's all there is to it and he's paying for your education.'

She'd said no more, obviously thinking it was a bad idea to confess the details of her private life to her sixteen-year-old daughter, of marriage and the problems it caused. We spent the rest of the journey in silence, her staring out of the window and me sending texts to Suki and the others, until she turned to me and said, 'I'll drop Greg once you leave school. I ought to get a good settlement out of the divorce and will have saved enough for both of us to live comfortably.'

She was sacrificing her happiness to keep me at Helton!

Arriving at the Hall, she brought up the subject of what had happened to me on Pictapost. Thankfully, Greg was out playing squash.

'We'll talk properly tomorrow,' she said. 'I'll take you somewhere nice for lunch and you can tell me everything. You must be tired now. Why not have an early night?'

I agreed because I was wrecked. My unpacking could wait. Although I missed Suki, Rahma and Tasha, it was good being back in my own space, surrounded by my posters and knick-knacks. Tulip had given me a massive hug and I was glad to see her again, grateful she asked no questions, turning down my bed in silence and leaving me alone. I locked my door before undressing, to keep a certain person from walking in uninvited, and climbed into bed.

I woke in the night clutching my stomach in terrible pain and sensed trickling down below. *My period! What a relief!* I'd been frightened I was pregnant and during my recuperation in the san, I'd managed to get out of bed and steal a pregnancy-testing kit from the clinic cupboard. Matron had been called away to an emergency and carelessly left the key in the lock. Earlier that day, I'd overheard one of the Sixth Form weeping in her office explaining why she needed to take a test. I escaped to the privacy of the toilet and was relieved the result was negative, pushing the fact my period had failed to start out of my mind; according to what I read on Google, it was normal for a girl my age to go a few weeks and sometimes months without having one.

Taking a couple of painkillers and pressing a hot water bottle on my tummy normally shifted the pain fairly quickly. Not on this occasion: I'd already used three sanitary towels. Something was definitely wrong and I was scared I was dying.

I fell asleep and was woken up by an urgent need to go to the bathroom. I was sticky down below and shocked to find my pyjama bottoms and sheets were soaked in blood, thick and clumpy. I was frightened; what was it? I spent nearly half an hour on the toilet, groaning, my insides turned inside out. Severe pain and a throbbing sensation down below told me I had a big problem.

I stood up carefully, went to the bath and ran the hot tap, turning away from the toilet. It was obvious what had happened and it was sad. It was also for the best.

I had to hide everything, get rid of the pyjamas and sheets to prevent Tulip seeing them and telling Mum. I staggered naked to my bed, putting a towel between my legs, and stripped it. Unsurprisingly, the mattress also had a stain. I put the duvet over it, decide what to do later. I'd read somewhere that salt and cold water were good for blood stains. At all costs, I had to prevent Tulip coming in to remake my bed. I'd requested a wake-up call at eight-thirty and in around ten minutes she'd be knocking on the door with a mug of tea, calling me to breakfast. Good job I'd locked the door: she had a habit of knocking and walking in.

I stuffed the bloodied sheets and pyjamas into the back of my wardrobe to keep them out of sight. The rap on the door turned me to stone: Tulip!

'Cherry? I've brought you a cuppa.'

I bit my lip and kept quiet.

The doorknob rattled and Tulip's tone became more urgent. 'Cherry!'

Oh, hell! I'd better let her in!

'Sorry, Tulip, I'm not hungry.'

She put her cool hand on my forehead. 'What's wrong, *cariad?*'

'I've got terrible period pain. I'm going to have a bath, see if that helps to ease it a bit.'

'Do you have any painkillers and towels?'

'I've got plenty of towels, thanks, but I finished the painkillers.'

'Right, I'll get some Femosyn and bring you a round of toast and a fresh cuppa. You have to eat. I'll tell your mum you're poorly.'

Bugger!

Her footsteps died away and I dragged on my dressing-gown. Remembering the hand towel between my legs, I chucked that, my pyjamas and sheets into the bottom of my wardrobe and dug out another pair of sanitary towels from the bottom of my unpacked trunk, hoping to avoid any uncomfortable questions from Mum. I turned off the bath tap, ensured the toilet and bathroom floor were clear of any evidence, and within ten minutes there was another knock.

'I'm coming.' I called innocently. Wringing my hands together, I checked everything in the bedroom and bathroom was how it ought to have been, and unlocked the door.

'Cherry, love?' Mum entered, followed by Tulip carrying a tray of tea, toast and the packet of Femosyn period pain tablets, and put her arm around me. 'What's wrong?'

Watching Tulip put the tray on the bed sent my anxiety levels soaring.

'Oh, the usual, really bad period pain, Mum,' I said weakly. I suffered most months and there was no reason for her to suspect anything else was wrong.

'You're really pale, though, love. Is the pain very bad?'

'Yeah, it's bad enough.' I shied away from Tulip's curiosity. *Please hurry up and leave!*

'Take the Femosyn,' said Mum, 'have a long soak and stay in bed today. I'll pop up and see you later.'

She left the room and Tulip said calmly, 'I'll sort your bed and refill your hot water bottle.'

'No, Tulip, really, there's no need!' I pleaded, almost tripping over my feet and diving on her. Not quick enough: she'd already removed the tray, put it on the bedside table and stripped back the duvet.

'Oh, Cherry!' she gasped.

I fell into her arms and cried like a baby.

***

Tulip closed and locked the bedroom door and I ended up telling her everything.

'He did *what?*' she roared.

'Shush! Keep it down, Tulip!' I begged. 'You'll bring Mum here! This is between you and me! Shut up and listen for a minute.'

Hearing the story from beginning to end, and what had occurred at the bungalow, turned Tulip's face red and angry.

'You have to go to the police!'

'No!' I cried, grabbing her hands. 'I told Suki at school I wouldn't do that. She – she said she'd anonymously reported the drugs and I've not heard from the police. It probably means there's no evidence and I'm – I'm glad. Promise me you won't grass to Mum!'

'Cherry, you'll have to go to hospital...'

'What?'

'They'll have to examine you and – and they will probably need to do a little operation, to avoid infection. That's what – had to happen to me and that can't be kept from your mum, especially if you have to stay in overnight.' That was when I heard the story of how she'd had a miscarriage a few years ago and why she guessed I was having more than a painful, heavy period. 'You have to tell her, *cariad,* or let me. Trust me, you'll feel better if it's out in the open.'

Sobbing and shaking, I put restraining hands on her arm, not realising how hard I was squeezing.

'Tulip, I'm so sorry you went through it, too, but please keep Mum out of this. I'll kill you if you breathe a word to her!'

'And *she'll* kill *me* if I keep my gob shut and she finds out!' she snapped, wriggling her arm free. 'I'll lose my job. Do you want me to leave?'

I shook my head miserably. She sat down again and grabbed my hands, now calmer and kinder.

'Listen, it's fine to be scared, your mum will go mental, but you have to wise up to the situation. It's not your fault he did that to you and it doesn't matter how long ago it happened, he committed a terrible crime and has to pay for it. What if he does it to another girl? How do you know he already hasn't? And you said he's been trolling you on Pictapost; the police will sort him out. It'll be OK.' She kissed my cheek. 'You'll have me and your mum to help you through it all. Now, let me ring down to the breakfast room and we'll tell her together, shall we? Come on, it won't be that bad, honest.'

I wish I was dead.

Thirty-Two
Cherry and Adam

It was finally over.

The worst eight months of my life were behind me: Mum's torment, crying, screaming, verbally attacking Greg for sending me away to school and making me rely on Pictapost for company, raging at me for contacting Adam, dragging me to the police station, the interviews, the questions, my body and my clothes examined, preparation by solicitors and barristers, going to court and facing all those people – and seeing Adam in the dock, a small, frightened little boy I almost felt sorry for. He'd walked into the court flanked by a legal team and a couple, a big man in a dark suit and attractive, fair-haired woman dressed in a purple dress and navy jacket: Adam's parents. His mother looked pale and distraught and my heart went out to her. Our barrister warned me and Mum not to address them. Sensing Mum was itching to shout out, I put my hand gently on her arm and she pulled it away. We hadn't been on the same terms since Tulip had forced me to tell her the whole sordid story. Of course, she didn't blame me for the rape, she was hurt and angry that I'd allowed Adam into the bungalow and I suspected forgiveness was a long way off; Tulip's assurances that she'd get over it was no help whatsoever. Greg called me a tart, a slur on the name of Milborne and Mum had thrown a valuable vase at him, packed our stuff and we left that day for Gran and Granddad's, her last words to him being, 'You'll be hearing from my solicitor!' It was the one good thing to come out of the entire sorry business: finally, she'd left Greg, vowing to take him to the cleaners. He'd yelled that he was glad to see the back of such a lousy wife.

'I faked it, by the way!' she'd screamed back.

Ordinarily, I'd have laughed out loud at that. Not now. She'd suffered enough at his hands.

The problem staying at Gran and Granddad's was being in their bad books, too. It was no surprise Cara had grassed about the events at the bungalow! Gran had cried and Granddad had been livid. 'History repeating itself!' he'd bellowed, and that was how I found out Mum had got pregnant at fourteen by some lad at school and lost the baby. She'd been angry at Granddad for bringing that up.

'People in glass houses shouldn't throw stones!' Gran had snapped at Mum, and Mum had bitten back, 'At least I own up to my mistakes!'

'I was raped, you weren't,' I pointed out furiously.

'Yes, I know, love, and if I ever get my hands on the little toerag, I'll cut his balls off!'

The verdict was a huge relief. Adam was guilty of the charges of fraud, possession of illegal substances, grooming and rape, sentenced to two years in young offenders and told to pay back the money he'd conned out of me; the right verdict, our barrister said. Mum agreed and was satisfied; I thanked the barrister and said no more, for, in spite of everything, Adam was always going to be Danny to me, and I mourned for what might have been.

I was responsible for the mess I was in, that's what Mom and Dad declared. Seeing Cherry in the court lobby caused my anger to rise to the point where if I'd had the opportunity to kill her, I'd have taken it gladly. Her lip quivered and she turned away. My legal team, paid for by Dad's superiors, told us to swerve her and her parents. Fine by me! Mom had suggested writing a letter of apology to Cherry and her parents and had been warned not to.

'It's inadvisable,' our barrister had said. 'It will be interpreted as accepting responsibility. You cannot contact the other party under any circumstances whatsoever.'

'We won't,' Dad had said, glaring over at Cherry and her mom. He'd said plenty away from court. 'Lady Milborne! Some lady; and a whore for a daughter to boot! I see that rich stepdaddy of hers hasn't turned up, either.'

I had other things to concern me other than where Lord Milborne was. I quaked in the dock waiting for the verdict, realising I was doomed on being detained by a team of cops at the airport. At first, I thought my parents had called them, but it turned out the police had had a tip-off, leading to them investigating the allegations of me being in possession of drugs and committing a sexual assault. I was done for both of those and for fraud, a sentence of two years in a young offenders' facility being my punishment. The fallout went further: Dad announced he was going back to the States to a desk job. Mom informed him she was staying in England for the length of my sentence and Dad's view was, 'Whatever. Back in the States it's the military academy for him. I'll see to it his offences here don't follow him and it'll teach him to stand on his own two feet, turn him into a man.'

Throughout my stint inside, he gave me a wide berth and we had little contact. Mom was taking daily antidepressants and changed towards me. I'd torn my family apart and I hated myself for it. Therapy was off the table now; there really was no going back from what I'd done.

All I had to keep me warm at night were dreams of Petrov and the casual relationships I formed in the unit, no one special, and not one of them held a candle to him. I missed enjoying his images on my cell. We weren't allowed phones and I had no clue what Scott and Dean were up to, whether they were aware of my disgrace. Probably not; my name had been kept out of the press for legal reasons. Mom had said Scott had been in touch, wondering why I hadn't turned up in New Jersey, and she'd told him I'd changed my mind about going back. I fretted Scott would be angry I'd messed him around and worried we might never see or speak to one another again.

The day Mom brought Petrov's letter on one of her infrequent visits was the happiest and scariest of my life. She'd already opened it and read the contents, explaining it was unit rules, and asked me what our relationship had been. Feeling I had nothing more to lose, I confessed everything. She was kind and promised to send my letters on to Petrov if I wanted to write back, agreeing not to disclose my wrongdoings to him. I was grateful and the moment he and I were reunited a few weeks on from my release was the highlight of my life.

Two years later, sitting in the military barber's chair getting my hair cut, I had one thing on my mind: somehow, some day, Cherry Hill was gonna pay.

Tulip, having left her job at the Hall, sat cross-legged on the floor of her room in the house she shared with other students, phone in hand.

'Right,' she murmured, 'goodbye and well done!' All her fake Pictapost accounts disappeared one by one. 'Let's hope I won't need to see you again.'

She studied a screenshot of the man she'd met on Tinder, a bitter reminder of how she'd been charmed by an older man at fifteen, who'd got her pregnant and shared her naked photos around social media. He'd also been a fraud, using a false name. On finding out his real name and his address, Tulip had written to his wife and sent photos of them together. She'd also gone to the police, leading him to be tried and convicted, labelled a paedophile, jailed, and added to the sex offenders' register. Revenge had been sweet then and it was sweet now. When Cherry had told her about Danny, Tulip had become suspicious of him straightaway and Ceridwen was born. Cherry was almost like a little sister to her and the prospect of her being hurt the way Tulip had been hurt was unbearable. It was upsetting she'd been unable to prevent what had happened to Cherry, but Cherry was now an older and wiser girl. She'd never be fooled like that again and Adam/Danny was condemned to the painful annals of her past.

Hearing footsteps, Tulip hastily put the phone away and stood up. She opened the door to the knock and Cherry was standing outside in her coat.

'Hi, Tulip, fancy a coffee?'

'Great idea.' Tulip smiled. 'I'll grab my jacket.'

They also treated themselves to a slice of chocolate cake each, discussing school and university. Sipping her latte, Tulip raised a silent toast to her Pictapost alter ego, the Welsh enchantress, Ceridwen.

www.ingramcontent.com/pod-product-compliance
Lightning Source LLC
LaVergne TN
LVHW010058170826
845678LV00012B/2162

* 9 7 8 0 9 5 5 8 5 5 0 5 4 *